Thomas Paine

From the portrait by Francois Bonneville. This portrait was painted while Paine was a member of the French National Convention.

The Life and Works
of
Thomas Paine

𝕻atriots' 𝕰dition

Edited by

William M. Van der Weyde

Volume VII

New Rochelle, New York
Thomas Paine National Historical Association
1925

CONTENTS

RIGHTS OF MAN, CONCLUDED
MISCELLANEOUS ESSAYS

RIGHTS OF MAN—PART SECOND

CHAPTER V

WAYS AND MEANS OF IMPROVING THE CONDITION OF EUROPE, INTERSPERSED WITH MISCELLANEOUS OBSERVATIONS.

THIS concluding chapter of the second part of the "Rights of Man," which placed Paine at the head of contemporary political writers, was published in February, 1792. Its popular reception established a precedent, nearly a million and a half copies being printed and published in England in the author's lifetime.

Naturally it made him enemies in government circles, and in September of that year he went to France by invitation of the French Convention. In December an English court found him guilty of treason for having written the revolutionary treatise, the publishers and booksellers being each sentenced to three years in prison. One of them, Thomas Clio Rickman, who afterwards wrote a life of Paine, avoided imprisonment by hurriedly following Paine to France.

IN contemplating a subject t h a t embraces with equatorial magnitude the w h o l e region of humanity, it is impossible to confine the pursuit in one single direction. It takes ground on every character and condition that appertains to man, and blends the individual, the nation, and the world.

From a small spark kindled in America, a flame has arisen not to be extinguished. Without consuming, like the *Ultima Ratio Regum*, it winds its progress from nation to nation, and conquers by a

1

silent operation. Man finds himself changed, he scarcely perceives how. He acquires a knowledge of his rights by attending justly to his interest, and discovers in the event that the strength and powers of despotism consist wholly in the fear of resisting it, and that in order, *"to be free, it is sufficient that he wills it."*

Having in all the preceding parts of this work endeavored to establish a system of principles as a basis on which governments ought to be erected, I shall proceed in this to the ways and means of rendering them into practise. But in order to introduce this part of the subject with more propriety and stronger effect, some preliminary observations, deducible from or connected with those principles, are necessary.

Whatever the form or constitution of government may be, it ought to have no other object than the *general* happiness. When, instead of this, it operates to create and increase wretchedness in any of the parts of society, it is on a wrong system, and reformation is necessary.

Customary language has classed the condition of man under the two descriptions of civilized and uncivilized life. To the one it has ascribed felicity and affluence; to the other hardship and want. But, however our imagination may be impressed by painting and comparison, it is nevertheless true, that a great portion of mankind in what are called civilized countries, are in a state of poverty and wretchedness, far below the condition of an Indian. I speak not of one country, but of all. It is so in England, it is so all over Europe. Let us inquire into the cause.

It lies not in any natural defect in the principles of civilization, but in preventing those principles having an universal operation; the consequence of which is a perpetual system of war and expense, that drains the country, and defeats the general felicity of which civilization is capable.

All the European governments (France now excepted) are constructed not on the principle of universal civilization, but on the reverse of it. So far as those governments relate to each other, they are in the same condition as we conceive of savage, uncivilized life; they put themselves beyond the law as well of God as of man, and are, with respect to principle and reciprocal conduct, like so many individuals in a state of nature.

The inhabitants of every country, under the civilization of laws, easily associate together, but governments being yet in an uncivilized state, and almost continually at war, they pervert the abundance which civilized life produces to carry on the uncivilized part to a greater extent.

By thus ingrafting the barbarism of government upon the internal civilization of a country, it draws from the latter, and more especially from the poor, a great portion of those earnings which should be applied to their own subsistence and comfort. Apart from all reflections of morality and philosophy it is a melancholy fact, that more than one-fourth of the labor of mankind is annually consumed by this barbarous system. What has served to continue this evil, is the pecuniary advantage which all the governments of Europe have found in keeping up this state of uncivilization. It affords to them pretenses for power and revenue, for which there would be neither occasion nor apology, if the circle of civilization were rendered complete.

Civil government alone, or the government of laws, is not productive of pretenses for many taxes; it operates at home, directly under the eye of the country, and precludes the possibility of much imposition. But when the scene is laid in the uncivilized contention of governments, the field of pretenses is enlarged, and the country, being no longer a judge, is open to every imposition, which governments please to act.

Not a thirtieth, scarcely a fortieth, part of the taxes which are raised in England are either occasioned by, or applied, to the purposes of civil government. It is not difficult to see that the whole which the actual government does in this respect is to enact laws, and that the country administers and executes them, at its own expense, by means of magistrates, juries, sessions, and assize, over and above the taxes which it pays.

In this view of the case, we have two distinct characters of government; the one, the civil government, or the government of laws, which operates at home; the other, the court or cabinet government, which operates abroad, on the rude plan of uncivilized life; the one attended with little charge, the other with boundless extravagance; and so distinct are the two, that if the latter were to sink, as it were, by a sudden opening of the earth, and totally disappear, the former would not be deranged. It would still proceed, because it is the common interest of the nation that it should, and all the means are in practise.

Revolutions, then, have for their object a change in the moral condition of governments, and with this change the burden of public taxes will lessen, and civilization will be left to the enjoyment of that abundance of which it is now deprived.

In contemplating the whole of this subject, I extend my views into the department of commerce. In all my publications, where the matter would admit, I have been an advocate for commerce, because I am a friend to its effects. It is a pacific system, operating to unite mankind by rendering nations, as well as individuals, useful to each other. As to the mere theoretical reformation, I have never preached it up. The most effectual process is that of improving the condition of man by means of his interest; and it is on this ground that I take my stand.

If commerce were permitted to act to the universal extent it is capable of, it would extirpate the system of war, and produce a revolution in the uncivilized state of governments. The invention of commerce has arisen since those governments began, and is the greatest approach toward universal civilization, that has yet been made by any means not immediately flowing from moral principles.

Whatever has a tendency to promote the civil intercourse of nations by an exchange of benefits is a subject as worthy of philosophy as of politics. Commerce is no other than the traffic of two individuals, multiplied on a scale of numbers; and by the same rule that nature intended the intercourse of two, she intended that of all. For this purpose she has distributed the materials of manufacturers and commerce in various and distant parts of a nation and of the world; and as they cannot be procured by war so cheaply or so commodiously as by commerce, she has rendered the latter the means of extirpating the former.

As the two are nearly the opposites of each other, consequently the uncivilized state of European governments is injurious to commerce. Every kind of destruction or embarrassment serves to lessen the quantity, and it matters but little in what part of the commercial world the reduction begins. Like blood, it cannot be taken from any of the parts without being taken from the whole mass in circulation, and all partake of the loss. When the ability in any nation to buy is destroyed, it equally involves the seller. Could the government of England destroy the commerce of all other nations, she would most effectually ruin her own.

It is possible that a nation may be the carrier for the world, but she cannot be the merchant. She cannot be the seller and the buyer of her own merchandise. The ability to buy must reside out of herself; and, therefore, the prosperity of any commercial nation is regulated by the prosperity of the rest. If they are poor, she cannot be rich; and her condition, be it what it may, is an index of the height of the commercial tide in other nations.

That the principles of commerce, and its universal operation may be understood without understanding the practise, is a position that reason will not deny; and it is on this ground only that I argue the subject. It is one thing in the counting house, in the world it is another.

With respect to its operation, it must necessarily be contemplated as a reciprocal thing, that only one-half its power resides within the nation, and that the whole is as effectually destroyed by destroying the half that resides without, as if the destruction had been committed on that which is within, for neither can act without the other.

When in the last, as well as in the former wars, the commerce of England sunk, it was because the general quantity was lessened everywhere; and it now rises because commerce is in a rising state in every nation. If England, at this day, imports or exports more than at any former period, the nations with which she trades must necessarily do the same; her imports are their exports, and *vice versa*.

There can be no such thing as a nation flourishing alone in commerce; she can only participate; and the destruction of it in any part must necessarily affect all. When, therefore, governments are at war, the attack is made upon the common stock of commerce, and the consequence is the same as if each had attacked his own.

The present increase of commerce is not to be attributed to ministers, or to any political contrivances, but to its own natural operations in consequence of peace. The regular markets have been destroyed, the channels of trade broken up, the high road of the seas infested with robbers of every nation, and the attention of the world called to other objects. Those interruptions have ceased, and peace has restored the deranged condition of things to their proper order.*

It is worth remarking that every nation reckons the balance of trade in its own favor; and therefore something must be irregular in the common ideas upon this subject.

The fact, however, is true, according to what is called a balance; and it is from this cause that com-

---

* In America the increase of commerce is greater in proportion than in England. It is, at this time, at least one-half more than at any period prior to the Revolution. The greatest number of vessels cleared out of the port of Philadelphia, before the commencement of the war was between eight and nine hundred. In the year 1788, the number was upwards of twelve hundred. As the State of Pennsylvania is estimated as an eighth part of the United States in population, the whole number of vessels must now be nearly ten thousand.—*Author.*

merce is universally supported. Every nation feels
the advantage, or it would abandon the practise: but
the deception lies in the mode of making up the
accounts, and attributing what are called profits to
a wrong cause.

Mr. Pitt has sometimes amused himself, by showing what he called a balance of trade from the custom-
house books. This mode of calculation, not only
affords no rule that is true, but one that is false.

In the first place, every cargo that departs from
the custom-house, appears on the books as an ex-
port; and according to the custom-house balance, the
losses at sea, and by foreign failures, are all reckoned
on the side of profit, because they appear as exports.

Secondly, Because the importation by the smug-
gling trade does not appear on the custom-house
books to arrange against the exports.

No balance, therefore, as applying to superior
advantages, can be drawn from these documents; and
if we examine the natural operation of commerce, the
idea is fallacious; and if true, would soon be injurious.
The great support of commerce consists in the balance
being a level of benefits among all nations.

Two merchants of different nations trading together, will both become rich, and each makes the
balance in his own favor; consequently, they do not

get rich out of each other; and it is the same with respect to the nations in which they reside. The case must be, that each nation must get rich out of its own means, and increases that riches by something it procures from another in exchange.

If a merchant in England sends an article of English manufacture abroad, which costs him a shilling at home, and imports something which sells for two, he makes a balance of one shilling in his own favor; but this is not gained out of the foreign nation, or the foreign merchant, for he also does the same by the article he receives, and neither has a balance of advantage upon the other.

The original value of the two articles in their proper countries was but two shillings; but by changing their places, they acquire a new idea of value, equal to double what they had at first, and that increased value is equally divided.

There is not otherwise a balance on foreign than on domestic commerce. The merchants of London and Newcastle trade on the same principles as if they resided in different nations, and make their balances in the same manner: yet London does not get rich out of Newcastle, any more than Newcastle out of London: but coals, the merchandise of Newcastle, have an additional value at London, and London merchandise has the same at Newcastle.

Though the principle of all commerce is the same, the domestic, in a national view, is the part the most beneficial; because the whole of the advantages, on both sides, rests within the nation; whereas, in foreign commerce, it is only a participation of one-half.

The most unprofitable of all commerce is that connected with foreign dominion. To a few individuals it may be beneficial, merely because it is commerce; but to the nation it is a loss. The expense of maintaining dominion more than absorbs the profits of any trade. It does not increase the general quantity in the world, but operates to lessen it; and as a greater mass would be afloat by relinquishing dominion, the participation without the expense would be more valuable than a greater quantity with it.

But it is impossible to engross commerce by dominion; and therefore it is still more fallacious. It cannot exist in confined channels, and necessarily breaks out by regular or irregular means that defeat the attempt, and to succeed would be still worse. France, since the Revolution, has been more than indifferent as to foreign possessions; and other nations will become the same, when they investigate the subject with respect to commerce.

To the expense of dominion is to be added that of navies, and when the amount of the two is subtracted from the profits of commerce, it will appear that what is called the balance of trade, even admitting it to exist, is not enjoyed by the nation, but absorbed by the government.

The idea of having navies for the protection of commerce is delusive. It is putting the means of destruction for the means of protection. Commerce needs no other protection than the reciprocal interest which every nation feels in supporting it—it is common stock—it exists by a balance of advantages to all; and the only interruption it meets, is from the present uncivilized state of governments, and which is its common interest to reform.*

Quitting this subject, I now proceed to other matters. As it is necessary to include England in the prospect of a general reformation, it is proper to

---

* When I saw Mr. Pitt's mode of estimating the balance of trade, in one of his parliamentary speeches, he appeared to me to know nothing of the nature and interest of commerce; and no man has more wantonly tortured it than himself. During a period of peace, it has been shackled with the calamities of war. Three times has it been thrown into stagnation, and the vessels unmanned by impressing, within less than four years of peace. —*Author.*

inquire into the defects of its government. It is only by each nation reforming its own, that the whole can be improved, and the full benefit of reformation enjoyed. Only partial advantages can flow from partial reforms. France and England are the only two countries in Europe where a reformation in government could have successfully begun. The one secure by the ocean, and the other by the immensity of its internal strength, could defy the malignancy of foreign despotism. But it is with revolutions as with commerce, the advantages increase by their becoming general, and double to either what each would receive alone.

As a new system is now opening to the view of the world, the European courts are plotting to counteract it. Alliances, contrary to all former systems, are agitating, and a common interest of courts is forming against the common interest of man.

This combination draws a line that runs throughout Europe, and presents a case so entirely new as to exclude all calculations from former circumstances. While despotism warred with despotism, man had no interest in the contest; but in a cause that unites the soldier with the citizen, and nation with nation, the despotism of courts, though it feels the danger, and meditates revenge, is afraid to strike.

No question has arisen within the records of history that pressed with the importance of the present. It is not whether this or that party shall be in or out, or Whig or Tory, or high or low shall prevail; but whether man shall inherit his rights, and universal civilization take place? Whether the fruits of his labor shall be enjoyed by himself, or consumed by the profligacy of governments? Whether robbery shall be banished from courts, and wretchedness from countries;

When, in countries that are called civilized, we see age going to the work-house, and youth to the gallows, something must be wrong in the system of government. It would seem, by the exterior appearance of such countries, that all was happiness; but there lies hidden from the eye of common observation, a mass of wretchedness that has scarcely any other chance than to expire in poverty or infamy. Its entrance into life is marked with the presage of its fate; and until this is remedied, it is in vain to punish.

Civil government does not consist in executions; but in making that provision for the instruction of youth, and the support of age, as to exclude, as much as possible, profligacy from the one, and despair from the other. Instead of this, the resources of a country are lavished upon kings, upon courts, upon hirelings, impostors, and prostitutes; and even the poor themselves, with all their wants upon them, are compelled to support the fraud that oppresses them.

Why is it that scarcely any are executed but the poor? The fact is a proof, among other things, of a wretchedness in their condition. Bred up without morals, and cast upon the world without a prospect, they are the exposed sacrifice of vice and legal barbarity. The millions that are superfluously wasted upon governments are more than sufficient to reform those evils, and to benefit the condition of every man in the nation, not included within the purlieus of a court. This I hope to make appear in the progress of this work.

It is the nature of compassion to associate with misfortune. In taking up this subject, I seek no recompense—I fear no consequences. Fortified with that proud integrity that disdains to triumph or to yield, I will advocate the Rights of Man.

At an early period, little more than sixteen years of age, raw and adventurous, and heated with the false heroism of a master* who had served in a man-of-war, I began the carver of my own fortune, and entered on board the *Terrible* privateer, Captain

---

* Rev. William Knowles, master of the grammar school at Thetford, in Norfolk.—*Author.*

Death. From this adventure I was happily prevented by the affectionate and moral remonstrance of a good father, who, from his own habits of life, being of the Quaker profession, must have begun to look upon me as lost. But the impression, much as it effected at the time, began to wear away, and I entered afterwards in the *King of Prussia* privateer, Captain Mendez, and went in her to sea.

Yet, from such a beginning, and with all the inconveniences of early life against me, I am proud to say that with a perseverance undismayed by difficulties, a disinterestedness that compelled respect, I have not only contributed to raise a new empire in the world, founded on a new system of government, but I have arrived at an eminence in political literature, the most difficult of all lines to succeed and excel in, which aristocracy, with all its aids, has not been able to reach or to rival.

Knowing my own heart, and feeling myself, as I now do, superior to all the skirmish of party, the inveteracy of interested or mistaken opponents, I answer not to falsehood or abuse, but proceed to the defects of the English Government.*

---

* Politics and self-interest have been so uniformly connected, that the world, from being so often deceived, has a right to be suspicious of public characters: but with regard to myself, I am

I begin with charters and corporations.

It is a perversion of terms to say that a charter gives rights. It operates by a contrary effect, that of taking rights away. Rights are inherently in all the inhabitants; but charters, by annulling those rights in the majority, leave the right, by exclusion, in the hands of a few. If charters were constructed so as

---

perfectly easy on this head. I did not, at my first setting out in public life, nearly seventeen years ago, turn my thoughts to subjects of government from motives of interest; and my conduct from that moment to this, proves the fact. I saw an opportunity, in which I thought I could do some good, and I followed exactly what my heart dictated. I neither read books, nor studied other people's opinions. I thought for myself. The case was this:

During the suspension of the old governments in America, both prior to and at the breaking out of hostilities, I was struck with the order and decorum with which everything was conducted; and impressed with the idea, that a little more than what society naturally performed, was all the government that was necessary, and that monarchy and aristocracy were frauds and impositions upon mankind.

On these principles I published the pamphlet "Common Sense." The success it met with was beyond anything since the invention of printing. I gave the copy-right to every State in the Union, and the demand ran to not less than one hundred thousand copies. I continued the subject in the same manner, under the title of the "Crisis," till the complete establishment of the Revolution.

After the Declaration of Independence, Congress, unanimously and unknown to me, appointed me secretary in the Foreign Department. This was agreeable to me because it gave me an opportunity of seeing into the abilities of foreign courts, and their manner of doing business. But a misunderstanding arising between Congress and me, respecting one of their commissioners, then in Europe, Mr. Silas Deane, I resigned the office, and de-to express in direct terms, *"that every inhabitant, who is not a member of a corporation, shall not exercise the right of voting,"* such charters would in the face be charters, not of rights, but of exclusion. The effect is the same under the form they now stand; and the only persons on whom they operate, are the persons whom they exclude.

---

clined, at the same time, the pecuniary offers made me by the Ministers of France and Spain, M. Gerard and Don Juan Mirralles.

I had by this time so completely gained the ear and confidence of America, and my independence was become so visible, as to give me a range of political writings, beyond, perhaps, what any man ever possessed in any country; and what is more extraordinary, I held it undiminished to the end of the war, and enjoy it in the same manner to the present moment. As my object was not myself, I set out with the determination, and happily with the disposition, of not being moved by praise or censure, friendship or calumny, nor of being drawn from my purpose by any personal altercation; and the man who cannot do this, is not fit for a public character.

When the war ended, I went from Philadelphia to Bordentown, on the East bank of the Delaware, where I have a small place. Congress was at this time at Princeton, fifteen miles distant; and General Washington had taken his head-quarters at Rocky Hill, within the neighborhood of Congress, for the purpose of resigning his commission (the object for which he accepted it being accomplished) and of retiring to private life. While he was on this business, he wrote me the letter which I here subjoin.

Rocky Hill, Sept. 10, 1783.

I have learned since I have been at this place, that you are at Bordentown. Whether for the sake of retirement or economy, I know not. Be it for either, for both, or whatever it may, if you

Those whose rights are guaranteed, by not being taken away, exercise no other rights than as members of the community they are entitled to without a charter; and, therefore, all charters have no other than an indirect negative operation. They do not give rights to A, but they make a difference in favor

will come to this place, and partake with me, I shall be exceedingly happy to see you.

Your presence may remind Congress of your past services to this country; and if it is in my power to impress them, command my best exertions with freedom, as they will be rendered cheerfully by one, who entertains a lively sense of the importance of your works, and who, with much pleasure, subscribes himself,

Your sincere friend,   G. WASHINGTON.

During the war, in the latter end of the year 1780, I formed to myself the design of coming over to England, and communicated it to General Greene, who was then in Philadelphia, on his route to the Southward, General Washington being then at too great a distance to communicate with immediately. I was strongly impressed with the idea, that, if I could get over to England, without being known, and only remain in safety till I could get out a publication, I could open the eyes of the country with respect to the madness and stupidity of its government. I saw that the parties in Parliament had pitted themselves as far as they could go, and could make no new impressions on each other. General Greene entered fully into my views, but the affair of Arnold and André happening just after, he changed his mind, and, under strong apprehensions for my safety, wrote very pressingly to me from Annapolis, in Maryland, to give up the design, which, with some reluctance, I did.

Soon after this I accompanied Colonel Laurens, (son of Mr. Laurens, who was then in the Tower), to France, on business from Congress. We landed at L'Orient, and while I remained of A, by taking away the rights of B, and consequently are instruments of injustice.

But charters and corporations have a more extensive evil effect than what relates merely to elections. They are sources of endless contention in the places where they exist; and they lessen the common rights

there, he being gone forward, a circumstance occurred that renewed my former design. An English packet from Falmouth to New York, with government despatches on board, was brought into L'Orient.

That a packet should be taken, is no very extraordinary thing, but that the despatches should be taken with it, will scarcely be credited, as they are always slung at the cabin window, in a bag loaded with cannon ball and ready to be sunk in a moment. The fact, however, is as I have stated it, for the despatches came into my hands, and I read them.

The capture, as I was informed, succeeded by the following stratagem:—The captain of the privateer *Madame*, who spoke English, on coming up with the packet, passed himself for the captain of an English frigate, and invited the captain of the packet on board, which, when done, he sent some of his own hands and secured the mail. But be the circumstance of the capture what it may, I speak with certainty as to the government despatches. They were sent up to Paris to Count Vergennes, and when Colonel Laurens and myself returned to America, we took the originals to Congress.

By these despatches I saw into the stupidity of the English Cabinet far more than I otherwise could have done, and I renewed my former design. But Colonel Laurens was so unwilling to return alone, more especially, as among other matters, he had a charge of upwards of two hundred thousand pounds sterling in money, that I gave in to his wishes, and finally gave up my plan. But I am now certain, that if I could have executed it, it would not have been altogether unsuccessful.—*Author.*

of national society. A native of England, under the operation of these charters and corporations, cannot be said to be an Englishman in the full sense of the word. He is not free of the nation, in the same manner that a Frenchman is free of France, and an American of America.

His rights are circumscribed to the town, and, in some cases, to the parish of his birth; and all other parts, though in his native land, are to him as a foreign country. To acquire a residence in these, he must undergo a local naturalization by purchase, or he is forbidden or expelled the place. This species of feudality is kept up to aggrandize the corporations at the ruin of the towns; and the effect is visible.

The generality of corporation towns are in a state of solitary decay, and prevented from further ruin only by some circumstance in their situation, such as a navigable river, or a plentiful surrounding country. As population is one of the chief sources of wealth, (for without it, land itself has no value), every thing which operates to prevent it, must lessen the value of property; and as corporations have not only this tendency, but directly this effect, they cannot but be injurious.

If any policy were to be followed, instead of that of general freedom, to every person to settle where he chose, (as in France or in America), it would be more consistent to give encouragement to new comers, than to preclude their admission by exacting premiums from them.*

The persons most immediately interested in the abolition of corporations, are the inhabitants of the towns where corporations are established. The instances of Manchester, Birmingham and Sheffield, show, by contrast, the injury which those Gothic institutions are to property and commerce. A few examples may be found, such as that of London, whose natural and commercial advantages, owing to its situation on the Thames, is capable of bearing up against the political evils of a corporation; but in almost all other cases the fatality is too visible to be doubted or denied.

---

* It is difficult to account for the origin of charter and corporation towns, unless we suppose them to have arisen out of, or having been connected with some species of garrison services. The times in which they began justify this idea. The generality of those towns have been garrisons, and the corporations were charged with the care of the gates of the town, when no military garrison was present. Their refusing or granting admission to strangers, which has produced the custom of giving, selling, and buying freedom, has more of the nature of garrison authority than civil government. Soldiers are free of all corporations throughout the nation, by the same propriety that every soldier is free of every garrison, and no other persons are. He can follow any employment, with the permission of his officers, in any corporation town throughout the nation.—*Author.*

Though the whole nation is not so directly affected
by the depression of property in corporation towns as
the inhabitants themselves, it partakes of the consequences. By lessening the value of property, the
quantity of national commerce is curtailed. Every
man is a customer in proportion to his ability; and
as all parts of a nation trade with each other, whatever affects any of the parts must necessarily communicate to the whole.

As one of the Houses of the English Parliament
is, in a great measure, made up by elections from
these corporations; and as it is unnatural that a pure
stream should flow from a foul fountain, its vices are
but a continuation of the vices of its origin. A man
of moral honor and good political principles, cannot
submit to the mean drudgery and disgraceful arts, by
which such elections are carried. To be a successful
candidate, he must be destitute of the qualities that
constitute a just legislator: and being thus disciplined
to corruption by the mode of entering into Parliament, it is not to be expected that the representative
should be better than the man.

Mr. Burke, in speaking of the English representation, has advanced as bold a challenge as ever was
given in the days of chivalry. "Our representation,"
says he, "has been found *perfectly adequate to all*

the purposes for which a representation of the people can be desired or devised. I defy," continues he, "the enemies of our Constitution to show the contrary." This declaration from a man who has been in constant opposition to all the measures of Parliament the whole of his political life, a year or two excepted, is most extraordinary, and, comparing him with himself, admits of no other alternative, than that he acted against his judgment as a member, or has declared contrary to it as an author.

But it is not in the representation only that the defects lie, and therefore I proceed in the next place to aristocracy.

What is called the House of Peers is constituted on a ground very similar to that against which there is a law in other cases. It amounts to a combination of persons in one common interest. No reason can be given, why a house of legislation should be composed entirely of men whose occupation consists in letting landed property, than why it should be composed of those who hire, or of brewers, or bakers, or any other separate class of men.

Mr. Burke calls this House *"the great ground and pillar of security to the landed interest."* Let us examine this idea.

What pillar of security does the landed interest require, more than any other interest in the state, or what right has it to a distinct and separate representation from the general interest of a nation? The only use to be made of this power, (and which it has always made), is to ward off taxes from itself, and throw the burden upon such articles of consumption by which itself would be least affected. That this has been the consequence (and will always be the consequence of constructing governments on combinations), is evident, with respect to England, from the history of its taxes.

Notwithstanding taxes have increased and multiplied upon every article of common consumption, the land tax, which more particularly affects this "pillar," has diminished. In 1788, the amount of the land-tax was £1,950,000 which is half a million less than it produced almost a hundred years ago,* notwithstanding the rentals are in many instances doubled since that period.

Before the coming of the Hanoverians, the taxes were divided in nearly equal proportions between the land and articles of consumption, the land bearing rather the largest share; but since that era, nearly

* See Sir John Sinclair's "History of the Revenue." The land-tax in 1646 was £2,473,499.—*Author*.

thirteen millions annually of new taxes have been thrown upon consumption. The consequence of which has been a constant increase in the number and wretchedness of the poor, and in the amount of the poor-rates.

Yet here again the burden does not fall in equal proportions on the aristocracy with the rest of the community. Their residences, whether in town or country, are not mixed with the habitations of the poor. They live apart from distress, and the expense of relieving it. It is in the manufacturing towns and laboring villages that those burdens press the heaviest; in many of which it is one class of poor supporting another.

Several of the most heavy and productive taxes are so contrived as to give an exemption to this pillar, thus standing in its own defense. The tax upon beer brewed for sale does not affect the aristocracy, who brew their own beer free of this duty. It falls only on those who have not conveniency or ability to brew, and who must purchase it in small quantities.

But what will mankind think of the justice of taxation, when they know, that this tax alone, from which the aristocracy are from circumstances exempt, is nearly equal to the whole of the land-tax, being in the year 1788, (and it is not less now), £1,666,152, and with its proportion of the taxes on malt and hops, it exceeds it. That a single article thus partially consumed, and that chiefly by the working part, should be subject to a tax equal to that on the whole rental of a nation, is, perhaps, a fact not to be paralleled in the history of revenues.

This is one of the consequences resulting from a house of legislation composed on the ground of a combination of common interest; for whatever their separate politics as to parties may be, in this they are united. Whether a combination acts to raise the price of an article for sale, or the rate of wages; or whether it acts to throw taxes from itself upon another class of the community, the principle and the effect are the same; and if the one be illegal, it will be difficult to show that the other ought to exist.

It is no use to say that the taxes are first proposed in the House of Commons; for as the other House has always a negative, it can always defend itself; and it would be ridiculous to suppose that its acquiescence in the measures to be proposed were not understood beforehand. Besides which, it has obtained so much influence by borough traffic, and so many of its relations and connections are distributed on both sides of the Commons, as to give it, besides an absolute negative in the House, a preponderancy in the other, in all matters of common concern.

It is difficult to discover what is meant by the *landed interest*, if it does not mean a combination of aristocratical land-holders, opposing their own pecuniary interest to that of the farmer, and every branch of trade, commerce, and manufacture. In all other respects, it is the only interest that needs no partial protection. It enjoys the general protection of the world.

Every individual, high or low, is interested in the fruits of the earth; men, women, and children, of all ages and degrees, will turn out to assist the farmer, rather than a harvest should not be got in; and they will not act thus by any other property. It is the only one for which the common prayer of mankind is put up, and the only one that can never fail from the want of means. It is the interest, not of the policy, but of the existence of man, and when it ceases, he must cease to be.

No other interest in a nation stands on the same united support. Commerce, manufactures, arts, sciences and everything else, compared with this, are supported but in parts. Their prosperity or their decay has not the same universal influence. When the valleys laugh and sing, it is not the farmer only, but all creation that rejoices. It is a prosperity that excludes all envy; and this cannot be said of anything else.

Why then does Mr. Burke talk of this House of Peers, as the pillar of the landed interest? Were that pillar to sink into the earth, the same landed property would continue, and the same plowing, sowing and reaping would go on. The aristocracy are not the farmers who work the land, and raise the produce, but are the mere consumers of the rent; and when compared with the active world, are the drones, a seraglio of males, who neither collect the honey nor form the hive, but exist only for lazy enjoyment.

Mr. Burke, in his first essay, called aristocracy *"the Corinthian capital of polished society."* Toward completing the figure, he has now added the *pillar*, but still the base is wanting; and whenever a nation chooses to act a Samson, not blind, but bold, down goes the temple of Dagon, the Lords and the Philistines.

If a house of legislation is to be composed of men of one class, for the purpose of protecting a distinct interest, all the other interests, should have the same. The inequality as well as the burden of taxation, arises from admitting it in one case and not in all. Had there been a house of farmers, there had been no

game laws; or a house of merchants and manufacturers; the taxes had neither been so unequal nor so
excessive. It is from the power of taxation being in
the hands of those who can throw so great a part of it
from their own shoulders, that it has raged without
a check.

Men of small or moderate estates are more injured
by the taxes being thrown on articles of consumption,
than they are eased by warding it from landed property, for the following reasons:

First, They consume more of the productive tax-
able articles, in proportion to their property, than
those of large estates.

Secondly, Their residence is chiefly in towns, and
their property in houses; and the increase of the
poor-rates, occasioned by taxes on consumption, is
in much greater proportion than the land-tax has
been favored. In Birmingham, the poor-rates are
not less than seven shillings in the pound. From
this, as is already observed, the aristocracy are in a
great measure exempt.

These are but a part of the mischiefs flowing from
the wretched scheme of an house of peers.

As a combination, it can always throw a considerable portion of taxes from itself; and as an hereditary
house, accountable to nobody, it resembles a rotten

borough, whose consent is to be courted by interest. There are but few of its members who are not in some mode or other participators, or disposers of the public money. One turns a candle-holder, or a lord in waiting; another a lord of the bed-chamber, a groom of the stole, or any insignificant nominal office, to which a salary is annexed, paid out of the public taxes, and which avoids the direct appearance of corruption. Such situations are derogatory to the character of man; and where they can be submitted to, honor cannot reside.

To all these are to be added the numerous dependents, the long list of the younger branches and distant relations, who are to be provided for at the public expense: in short, were an estimation to be made of the charge of the aristocracy to a nation, it will be found nearly equal to that of supporting the poor. The Duke of Richmond alone (and there are cases similar to his) takes away as much for himself as would maintain two thousand poor and aged persons. Is it, then, any wonder that under such a system of government, taxes and rates have multiplied to their present extent?

In stating these matters, I speak an open and disinterested language, dictated by no passion but that of humanity. To me, who have not only refused offers, because I thought them improper, but have declined rewards I might with reputation have accepted, it is no wonder that meanness and imposition appear disgusting. Independence is my happiness, and I view things as they are, without regard to place or person; my country is the world, and my religion is to do good.

Mr. Burke, in speaking of the aristocratical law of primogeniture, says, "It is the standard law of our landed inheritance; and which, without question has a tendency, and I think," continues he, "a happy tendency to preserve a character of weight and consequence."

Mr. Burke may call this law what he pleases, but humanity and impartial reflection will pronounce it a law of brutal injustice. Were we not accustomed to the daily practise, and did we only hear of it, as the law of some distant part of the world, we should conclude that the legislators of such countries had not yet arrived at a state of civilization.

As to its preserving a character of *weight and consequence,* the case appears to me directly the reverse. It is an attaint upon character; a sort of privateering upon family property. It may have weight among dependent tenants, but it gives none on a scale of national, and much less of universal character. Speak-

ing for myself, my parents were not able to give me
a shilling, beyond what they gave me in education;
and to do this they distressed themselves; yet I possess
more of what is called consequence, in the world than
any one in Mr. Burke's catalogue of aristocrats. Having thus glanced at some of the defects of the two
Houses of Parliament, I proceed to what is called the
Crown, upon which I shall be very concise.

It signifies a nominal office of a million sterling a
year, the business of which consists in receiving the
money. Whether the person be wise or foolish, sane
or insane, a native or a foreigner, matters not. Every
ministry acts upon the same idea that Mr. Burke
writes, namely, that the people must be hoodwinked,
and held in superstitious ignorance by some bugbear
or other; and what is called the Crown answers this
purpose, and therefore it answers all the purposes to
be expected from it. This is more than can be said
of the other two branches.

The hazard to which this office is exposed in all
countries is not from anything that can happen to the
man, but from what may happen to the nation,—the
danger of its coming to its senses.

It has been customary to call the Crown the executive power, and the custom has continued, though
the reason has ceased.

It was called the *executive,* because the person whom it signifies used, formerly, to sit in the character of a judge, in administering or executing the laws. The tribunals were then a part of the court. The power, therefore, which is now called the judicial, is what was called the executive; and, consequently, one or the other of the terms is redundant, and one of the offices useless. When we speak of the Crown, now, it means nothing; it signifies neither a judge nor a general; besides which, it is the laws that govern, and not the man. The old terms are kept up, and give an appearance of consequence to empty forms; and the only effect they have is that of increasing expenses.

Before I proceed to the means of rendering governments more conducive to the general happiness of mankind than they are at present, it will not be improper to take a review of the progress of taxation in England.

It is a general idea, that when taxes are once laid on, they are never taken off. However true this may have been of late, it was not always so. Either, therefore, the people of former times were more watchful over government than those of the present, or government was administered with less extravagance.

It is now seven hundred years since the Norman

Conquest, and the establishment of what is called the
Crown. Taking this portion of time in seven separate
periods of one hundred years each, the amount of
annual taxes, at each period, will be as follows:

Annual amount of taxes levied by William the Con-
    queror, beginning in the year 1066 . . . . . £400,000
Annual amount of taxes at one hundred years from the
    Conquest, (1166) 200,000
Annual amount of taxes at two hundred years from the
    Conquest, (1266) 150,000
Annual amount of taxes at three hundred years from
    the Conquest, (1366) 130,000
Annual amount of taxes at four hundred years from
    the Conquest, (1466) 100,000

These statements, and those which follow, are
taken from Sir John Sinclair's "History of the Revenue;" by which it appears that taxes continued decreasing for four hundred years, at the expiration of
which time they were reduced three-fourths, *viz.* from
four hundred thousand pounds to one hundred thousand. The people of England, of the present day,
have a traditionary and historical idea of the bravery
of their ancestors; but whatever their virtues or vices
might have been, they certainly were a people who
would not be imposed upon, and who kept government in awe as to taxation, if not as to principle.
Though they were not able to expel the monarchical

usurpation, they restricted it to a republican economy of taxes.

Let us now review the remaining three hundred years.

Annual amount of taxes at five hundred years from the Conquest, (1566)	£500,000
Annual amount of taxes at six hundred years from the Conquest, (1666)	1,800,000
Annual amount of taxes at the present time, (1791)	17,000,000

The difference between the first four hundred years and the last three, is so astonishing, as to warrant the opinion, that the national character of the English has changed. It would have been impossible to have dragooned the former English into the excess of taxation that now exists; and when it is considered that the pay of the army, the navy, and of all the revenue-officers, is the same now as it was above a hundred years ago, when the taxes were not above a tenth part of what they are at present, it appears impossible to account for the enormous increase and expenditure, on any other ground than extravagance, corruption, and intrigue.*

---

* Several of the court newspapers have of late made frequent mention of Wat Tyler. That his memory should be traduced by court sycophants, and all those who live on the spoil of a public, is not to be wondered at. He was, however, the means of checking the rage and injustice of taxation in his time, and the nation

With the Revolution of 1688, and more so since the Hanover Succession, came the destructive system of continental intrigues, and the rage of foreign wars and foreign dominion; systems of such secure mystery, that the expenses admit of no accounts; a single line stands for millions. To what excess taxation might have extended, had not the French Revolution contributed to break up the system, and put an end to pretenses, it is impossible to say.

Viewed as that revolution ought to be, as the fortunate means of lessening the load of taxes of both

---

owed much to his valor. The history is concisely this:—In the time of Richard II a poll-tax was levied, of one shilling per head, upon every person in the nation, of whatever estate or condition, on poor as well as rich, above the age of fifteen years.

If any favor was shown in the law, it was to the rich rather than to the poor; as no person could be charged more than twenty shillings for himself, family and servants, though ever so numerous; while all other families, under the number of twenty, were charged per head. Poll-taxes had always been odious; but this, being also oppressive and unjust, it excited, as it naturally must, universal detestation among the poor and middle classes.

The person known by the name of Wat Tyler, whose proper name was Walter, and a tyler by trade, lived at Deptford. The gatherer of the poll-tax, on coming to his house, demanded tax for one of his daughters, whom Tyler declared was under the age of fifteen. The tax-gatherer insisted on satisfying himself, and began an indecent examination of the girl, which enraging the father, he struck him with a hammer, that brought him to the ground, and was the cause of his death.

This circumstance served to bring the discontents to an issue. The inhabitants of the neighborhood espoused the cause of Tyler,

countries, it is of as much importance to England as
to France; and, if properly improved to all the advantages of which it is capable, and to which it leads,
deserves as much celebration in one country as the
other.

In pursuing this subject, I shall begin with the
matter that first presents itself, that of lessening the
burden of taxes; and shall then add such matters and
propositions, respecting the three countries of England, France, and America, as the present prospect of
things appears to justify; I mean an alliance of the

---

who in a few days was joined, according to some histories, by
upwards of fifty thousand men, and chosen their chief. With
this force he marched to London, to demand an abolition of the
tax, and a redress of their grievances. The court, finding itself
in a forlorn condition, and unable to make resistance, agreed,
with Richard at its head, to hold a conference with Tyler in
Smithfield, making many fair professions, courtier-like, of its
disposition to redress the oppressions.

While Richard and Tyler were in conversation on these matters, each being on horseback, Walworth, then Mayor of London,
and one of the creatures of the court, watched an opportunity,
and like a cowardly assassin, stabbed Tyler with a dagger; and
two or three others falling upon him, he was instantly sacrificed.

Tyler appears to have been an intrepid, disinterested man,
with respect to himself. All his proposals made to Richard, were
on a more just and public ground, than those which had been
made to John by the barons; and notwithstanding the sycophancy
of historians, and men like Mr. Burke, who seek to gloss over
a base action of the court by traducing Tyler, his fame will outlive their falsehood. If the barons merited a monument to be
erected in Runneymede, Tyler merits one in Smithfield.—*Author.*

three, for the purposes that will be mentioned in their proper place.

What has happened may happen again. By the statement before shown, of the progress of taxation, it is seen, that taxes have been lessened to a fourth part of what they had formerly been. Though the present circumstances do not admit of the same reduction, yet they admit of such a beginning, as may accomplish that end in a less time, than in the former case.

The amount of taxes for the year, ending at Michaelmas, 1788, was as follows:

Land tax	£1,950,000
Customs	3,789,274
Excise (including old and new malt)	6,751,727
Stamps	1,278,214
Miscellaneous taxes and incidents	1,803,755
	£15,572,970

Since the year 1788, upwards of one million, new taxes, have been laid on, besides the produce of the lotteries; and as the taxes have in general been more productive since than before, the amount may be taken, in round numbers, at £17,000,000.

N. B. The expense of collection and the drawbacks, which together amount to nearly two millions, are paid out of the gross amount; and the above is the net sum paid into the exchequer.

This sum of seventeen millions is applied to two different purposes; the one to pay the interest of the national debt, the other to pay the current expenses of each year. About nine millions are appropriated to the former; and the remainder, being nearly eight millions, to the latter. As to the million, said to be applied to the reduction of the debt, it is so much like paying with one hand and taking out with the other, as not to merit much notice.

It happened, fortunately for France, that she possessed national domains for paying off her debt, and thereby lessening her taxes; but as this is not the case in England, her reduction of taxes can only take place by reducing the current expenses, which may now be done to the amount of four or five millions annually, as will hereafter appear. When this is accomplished, it will more than counterbalance the enormous charge of the American War; and the saving will be from the same source from whence the evil rose.

As to the national debt, however heavy the interest may be in taxes, yet, as it serves to keep alive a capital, useful to commerce, it balances by its effects a considerable part of its own weight; and as the quantity of gold and silver in England is, by some means or other, short of its proper proportion* (being not more than twenty millions, whereas it should be sixty), it would, besides the injustice, be bad policy to extinguish a capital that serves to supply that defect. But, with respect to the current expense, whatever is saved therefrom is gain. The excess may serve to keep corruption alive, but it has no reaction on credit and commerce, like the interest of the debt.

It is now very probable, that the English Government (I do not mean the nation) is unfriendly to the French Revolution. Whatever serves to expose the intrigue and lessen the influence of courts, by lessening taxation, will be unwelcome to those who feed upon the spoil. Whilst the clamor of French intrigue, arbitrary power, popery, and wooden shoes, could be kept up, the nations were easily allured and alarmed into taxes. Those days are now past; deception, it is to be hoped, has reaped its last harvest, and better times are in prospect for both countries, and for the world.

Taking it for granted that an alliance may be formed between England, France and America, for the purposes hereafter to be mentioned, the national expenses of France and England may consequently be

---

* Foreign intrigues, foreign wars, and foreign dominions, will in a great measure account for the deficiency.—*Author.*

lessened. The same fleets and armies will no longer be necessary to either, and the reduction can be made ship for ship on each side. But to accomplish these objects, the governments must necessarily be fitted to a common correspondent principle. Confidence can never take place while a hostile disposition remains in either, or where mystery and secrecy on one side is opposed to candor and openness on the other.

These matters admitted, the national expenses might be put back, *for the sake of a precedent,* to what they were at some period when France and England were not enemies. This, consequently must be prior to the Hanover Succession, and also to the Revolution of 1688.* The first instance that presents itself,

---

* I happened to be in England at the celebration of the centenary of the Revolution of 1688. The characters of William and Mary have always appeared to me detestable; the one seeking to destroy his uncle, and the other her father, to get possession of power themselves: yet, as the nation was disposed to think something of that event, I felt hurt at seeing it ascribe the whole reputation of it to a man who had undertaken it as a job, and who, besides what he otherwise got, charged £600,000 for the expense of the little fleet that brought him from Holland.

George I acted the same close-fisted part as William had done, and bought the Duchy of Bremen with the money he got from England, two hundred and fifty thousand pounds over and above his pay as king; and having thus purchased it at the expense of England, added it to his Hanoverian dominions for his own private benefit. In fact, every nation that does not govern itself, is governed as a job. England has been the prey of jobs ever since the Revolution.—*Author.*

antecedent to those dates, is in the very wasteful and profligate times of Charles II, at which time England and France acted as allies. If I have chosen a period of great extravagance, it will serve to show modern extravagance in a still worse light; especially, as the pay of the navy, the army, and the revenue-officers has not increased since that time.

The peace establishment was then as follows: (See Sir John Sinclair's "History of the Revenue").

Navy	£300,000
Army	212,000
Ordnance	40,000
Civil List	462,115
	£1,014,115

The Parliament, however, settled the whole annual peace establishment of £1,200,000.* If we go back to the time of Elizabeth, the amount of all the taxes was but half a million, yet the nation sees nothing, during that period, that reproaches it with want of consequence.

All circumstances, then, taken together, arising from the French Revolution, from the approaching

* Charles, like his predecessors and successors, finding that war was the harvest of governments, engaged in a war with the Dutch, the expense of which increased the annual expenditure to £1,800,000 as stated under the date of 1666; but the peace establishment was but £1,200,000.—*Author.*

harmony and reciprocal interest of the two nations, the abolition of court intrigue on both sides, and the progress of knowledge in the science of government, the annual expenditure might be put back to one million and a half, *viz.*

Navy	£500,000
Army	500,000
Expenses of government	500,000
	£1,500,000

Even this sum is six times greater than the expenses of government are in America, yet the civil internal government of England (I mean that administered by means of quarter-sessions, juries, and assize, and which, in fact, is nearly the whole, and is performed by the nation), is less expense upon the revenue, than the same species and portion of government is in America.

It is time that nations should be rational, and not be governed like animals for the pleasure of their riders. To read the history of kings, a man would be almost inclined to suppose that government consisted in stag-hunting, and that every nation paid a million a year to the huntsman. Man ought to have pride or shame enough to blush at being thus imposed upon, and when he feels his proper character, he will.

Upon all subjects of this nature, there is often passing in the mind a train of ideas he has not yet accustomed himself to encourage and communicate. Restrained by something that puts on the character of prudence, he acts the hypocrite upon himself as well as to others. It is, however, curious to observe how soon this spell can be dissolved. A single expression, boldly conceived and uttered, will sometimes put a whole company into their proper feelings, and whole nations are acted upon in the same manner.

As to the offices of which any civil government may be composed, it matters but little by what names they are described. In the routine of business, as before observed, whether a man be styled a president, a king, an emperor, a senator, or any thing else, it is impossible that any service he can perform, can merit from a nation more than ten thousand pounds a year; and as no man should be paid beyond his services, so every man of a proper heart will not accept more.

Public money ought to be touched with the most scrupulous consciousness of honor. It is not the produce of riches only, but of the hard earnings of labor and poverty. It is drawn even from the bitterness of want and misery. Not a beggar passes, or perishes in the streets, whose mite is not in that mass.

Were it possible that the Congress of America, could be so lost to their duty, and to the interest of their constituents, as to offer General Washington, as President of America, a million a year, he would not, and he could not accept it. His sense of honor is of another kind. It has cost England almost seventy millions sterling, to maintain a family imported from abroad, of very inferior capacity to thousands in the nation; and scarcely a year has passed that has not produced some new mercenary application. Even the physicians' bills have been sent to the public to be paid.

No wonder that jails are crowded, and taxes and poor-rates increased. Under such systems, nothing is to be looked for but what has already happened; and as to reformation, whenever it comes, it must be from the nation, and not from the government.

To show that the sum of five hundred thousand pounds is more than sufficient to defray all the expenses of government, exclusive of navies and armies, the following estimate is added for any country, of the same extent as England.

In the first place, three hundred representatives, fairly elected, are sufficient for all the purposes to which legislation can apply, and preferable to a larger number. They may be divided into two or three houses, or meet in one, as in France, or in any manner a constitution shall direct.

As representation is always considered in free countries as the most honorable of all stations, the allowance made to it is merely to defray the expenses which the representatives incur by that service, and not to it as an office.

If an allowance at the rate of five hundred pounds
    per annum be made to every representative, de-
    ducting for non-attendance, the expense, if the whole
    number attended for six months each year would be   £75,000
The official departments cannot reasonably exceed the
    following number, with the salaries annexed:
Three offices, at ten thousand pounds each   30,000
Ten ditto, at five thousand pounds each   50,000
Twenty ditto, at two thousand pounds each . . .   40,000
Forty ditto, at one thousand pounds each   40,000
Two hundred ditto, at five hundred pounds each . . 100,000
Three hundred ditto, at two hundred pounds each .   60,000
Five hundred ditto, at one hundred pounds each . .   50,000'
Seven hundred ditto, at seventy-five pounds each . .   52,500

                                                ————
                                              £497,500

If a nation chooses, it can deduct four per cent from all offices, and make one of twenty thousand per annum.

All revenue-officers are paid out of the monies they collect, and therefore, are not included in this estimation.

The foregoing is not offered as an exact detail of offices, but to show the number and rate of salaries which five hundred thousand pounds will support; and it will, on experience, be found impracticable to find business sufficient to justify even this expense. As to the manner in which office business is now performed, the chiefs in several offices, such as the post-office, and certain offices in the exchequer, etc., do little more than sign their names three or four times a year; and the whole duty is performed by under-clerks.

Taking, therefore, one million and a half as a sufficient peace establishment for all the honest purposes of government, which is three hundred thousand pounds more than the peace establishment in the profligate and prodigal times of Charles II (notwithstanding, as has been already observed, the pay and salaries of the army, navy, and revenue-officers, continue the same as at that period), there will remain a surplus of upwards of six millions out of the present current expenses. The question then will be, how to dispose of this surplus.

Whoever has observed the manner in which trade and taxes twist themselves together, must be sensible of the impossibility of separating them suddenly.

First, Because the articles now on hand are already charged with the duty, and the reduction cannot take place on the present stock.

Secondly, Because, on all those articles on which the duty is charged in the gross, such as per barrel, hogshead, hundred weight, or ton, the abolition of the duty does not admit of being divided down so as fully to relieve the consumer, who purchases by the pint, or the pound. The last duty paid on strong beer and ale, was three shillings per barrel, which, if taken off, would lessen the purchase only half a farthing per pint, and consequently, would not reach to practical relief.

This being the condition of a greater part of the taxes, it will be necessary to look for such others as are free from this embarrassment, and where the relief will be direct and visible, and capable of immediate operation.

In the first place, then, the poor-rates are a direct tax which every housekeeper feels, and who knows also, to a farthing, the sum which he pays. The national amount of the whole of the poor-rates is not positively known, but can be procured. Sir John Sinclair in his "History of the Revenue," has stated it at £2,100,587, a considerable part of which is expended in litigations, in which the poor, instead of being relieved, are tormented. The expense, however, is the same to the parish, from whatever cause it arises.

In Birmingham, the amount of the poor-rates is fourteen thousand pounds a year. This, though a large sum, is moderate compared with the population. Birmingham is said to contain seventy thousand souls, and on a proportion of seventy thousand to fourteen thousand pounds poor-rates, the national amount of poor-rates, taking the population of England at seven millions, would be but one million four hundred thousand pounds. It is, therefore, most probable, that the population of Birmingham is over-rated. Fourteen thousand pounds is the proportion upon fifty thousand souls, taking two millions of poor-rates as the national amount.

Be it, however, what it may, it is no other than the consequence of the excessive burden of taxes, for, at the time when the taxes were very low, the poor were able to maintain themselves; and there were no poor-rates.* In the present state of things, a laboring man, with a wife and two or three children, does not pay less than between seven and eight poun

---

* Poor-rates began about the time of Henry VIII when taxes began to increase, and they have increased as the taxes increased ever since.—*Author.*

a year in taxes. He is not sensible of this, because it is disguised to him in the articles which he buys, and he thinks only of their dearness; but as the taxes take from him, at least, a fourth part of his yearly earnings, he is consequently disabled from providing for a family, especially if himself, or any of them, are afflicted with sickness.

The first step, therefore, of practical relief, would be to abolish the poor-rates entirely, and, in lieu thereof, to make a remission of taxes to the poor to double the amount of the present poor-rates, *viz.*, four millions annually out of the surplus taxes. By this measure, the poor would be benefited two millions, and the housekeepers two millions. This alone would be equal to a reduction of one hundred and twenty millions of the national debt, and consequently equal to the whole expense of the American War.

It will then remain to be considered, which is the most effectual mode of distributing the remission of four millions.

It is easily seen, that the poor are generally composed of large families of children, and old people unable to labor. If these two classes are provided for, the remedy will so far reach to the full extent of the case, that what remains will be incidental, and, in a great measure, fall within the compass of benefit clubs, which, though of humble invention, merit to be ranked among the best of modern institutions.

Admitting England to contain seven millions of souls; if one-fifth thereof are of that class of poor which need support, the number will be one million four hundred thousand. Of this number, one hundred and forty thousand will be aged poor, as will be hereafter shown, and for which a distinct provision will be proposed.

There will then remain one million two hundred and sixty thousand, which, at five souls to each family, amount to two hundred and fifty-two thousand families, rendered poor from the expense of children and the weight of taxes.

The number of children under fourteen years of age, in each of those families, will be found to be about five to every two families; some having two, others three; some one, and others four; some none, and others five; but it rarely happens that more than five are under fourteen years of age, and after this age they are capable of service, or of being apprenticed.

Allowing five children (under fourteen years) to every two families,

The number of children will be 630,000
The number of parents (were they all living) would
be 504,000

It is certain that if the children are provided for, the parents are relieved of consequence, because it is from the expense of bringing up children that their poverty arises.

Having thus ascertained the greatest number that can be supposed to need support on account of young families, I proceed to the mode of relief, or distribution, which is,

To pay as a remission of taxes to every poor family, out of the surplus taxes and in room of poor-rates, four pounds a year for every child under fourteen years of age; enjoining the parents of such children to send them to school, to learn reading, writing, and common arithmetic; the ministers of every parish, of every denomination, to certify jointly to an office, for this purpose, that the duty is performed. The amount of this expense will be:

For six hundred and thirty thousand children at
four pounds each per annum £2,520,000

By adopting this method, not only the poverty of the parents will be relieved, but ignorance will be banished from the rising generation, and the number of poor will hereafter become less, because their abilities, by the aid of education, will be greater. Many a youth, with good natural genius, who is apprenticed to a mechanical trade, such as a carpenter, joiner, millwright, blacksmith, etc., is prevented getting forward the whole of his life, from the want of a little common education when a boy.

I now proceed to the case of the aged.

I divide age into two classes. First, the approach of old age, beginning at fifty. Secondly, old age commencing at sixty.

At fifty, though the mental faculties of man are in full vigor, and his judgment better than at any preceding date, the bodily powers are on the decline. He cannot bear the same quantity of fatigue as at an earlier period. He begins to earn less, and is less capable of enduring the wind and weather; and in those retired employments where much sight is required, he fails apace, and feels himself like an old horse, beginning to be turned adrift.

At sixty, his labor ought to be over, at least from direct necessity. It is painful to see old age working itself to death, in what are called civilized countries, for its daily bread.

To form some judgment of the number of those above fifty years of age, I have several times counted the persons I met in the streets of London, men, women, and children, and have generally found that the average is one in about sixteen or seventeen. If it be said that aged persons do not come much into the streets, so neither do infants; and a great proportion of grown children are in schools, and in the work-shops as apprentices. Taking then sixteen for a divisor, the whole number of persons, in England, of fifty years and upwards, of both sexes, rich and poor, will be four hundred and twenty thousand.

The persons to be provided for out of this gross number will be husbandmen, common laborers, journeymen of every trade and their wives, sailors, and disbanded soldiers, worn-out servants of both sexes, and poor widows.

There will be also a considerable number of middling tradesmen, who, having lived decently in the former part of life, begin, as age approaches, to lose their business, and at last fall into decay.

Besides these, there will be constantly thrown off from the revolutions of that wheel, which no man can stop, nor regulate, a number from every class of life connected with commerce and adventure.

To provide for all those accidents, and whatever else may befall, I take the number of persons, who at one time or other of their lives, after fifty years of age, may feel it necessary or comfortable to be better supported, than they can support themselves, and that not as a matter of grace and favor, but of right, at one-third of the whole number, which is one hundred and forty thousand, as stated p. 53, and for whom a distinct provision was to be made. If there be more, society, notwithstanding the show and pomposity of government, is in a deplorable condition in England.

Of this one hundred and forty thousand, I take one-half, seventy thousand, to be of the age of fifty and under sixty, and the other half to be sixty years and upwards. Having thus ascertained the probable proportion of the number of aged persons, I proceed to the mode of rendering their condition comfortable, which is,

To pay to every such person of the age of fifty years, and until he shall arrive at the age of sixty, the sum of six pounds per annum out of the surplus taxes; and ten pounds per annum during life, after the age of sixty. The expense of which will be:

Seventy thousand persons at six pounds per annum	£420,000
Seventy thousand persons at ten pounds per annum	700,000
	£1,120,000

This support, as already remarked, is not of the nature of charity, but of a right. Every person in England, male or female, pays on an average of taxes, two pounds eight shillings and sixpence per annum from the day of his (or her) birth; and if the expense of collection be added, he pays two pounds, eleven shillings and sixpence; consequently, at the end of fifty years, he has paid one hundred and twenty-eight pounds fifteen shillings; and at sixty, one hundred and fifty-four pounds ten shillings.

Converting, therefore, his (or her) individual tax into a tontine, the money he shall receive after fifty years, is but little more than the legal interest of the net money he has paid; the rest is made up from those whose circumstances do not require them to draw such support, and the capital in both cases defrays the expenses of government.

It is on this ground that I have extended the probable claims to one-third of the number of aged persons in the nation. Is it then better that the lives of one hundred and forty thousand aged persons be rendered comfortable, or that a million a year of public money be expended on any one individual, and he often of the most worthless and insignificant character? Let reason and justice, let honor and humanity, let even hypocrisy, sycophancy, and Mr. Burke, let George, let Louis, Leopold, Frederic, Catherine, Cornwallis, or Tippoo Saib, answer the question.*

---

* Reckoning the taxes by families, five to a family, each family pays on an average £12 17 6 per annum: To this sum are to

The sum thus remitted to the poor will be:

To two hundred and fifty-two thousand poor families, containing six hundred and thirty thousand children	£2,520,000
To one hundred and fifty thousand aged persons .	1,120,000
	£3,640,000

There will then remain three hundred and sixty thousand pounds out of the four millions, part of which may be applied as follows:

After all the above cases are provided for, there will still be a number of families who, though not properly of the class of poor, yet find it difficult to give education to their children, and such children,

be added the poor-rates. Though all pay taxes in the articles they consume, all do not pay poor-rates. About two millions are exempted, some as not being housekeepers, others as not being able, and the poor themselves who receive the relief. The average, therefore, of poor-rates on the remaining number, is forty shillings for every family of five persons, which makes the whole average amount of taxes and rates £14 17 6. For six persons, £17 17. For seven persons, £20 16 6.

The average of taxes in America, under the new or representative system of government, including the interest of the debt contracted in the war, and taking the population at four millions of souls, which it now amounts to, and is daily increasing, is five shillings per head, men, women and children. The difference, therefore, between the two governments, is as under:

	England.	America.
For a family of five persons . . .	£14 17 6	£1 5 0
For a family of six persons . . .	17 17 0	1 10 0
For a family of seven persons . .	20 16 6	1 15 0

—*Author.*

under such a case, would be in a worse condition than if their parents were actually poor. A nation under a well regulated government should permit none to remain uninstructed. It is monarchial and aristocratical governments, only, that require ignorance for their support.

Suppose then four hundred thousand children to be in this condition, which is a greater number than ought to be supposed, after the provisions already made, the method will be:

To allow for each of those children ten shillings a year for the expense of schooling, for six years each, which will give them six months schooling each year, and half a crown a year for paper and spelling books.

The expense of this will be annually * £250,000.

---

* Public schools do not answer the general purpose of the poor. They are chiefly in corporation-towns, from which the country towns and villages are excluded; or, if admitted, the distance occasions a great loss of time. Education, to be useful to the poor, should be on the spot; and the best method, I believe, to accomplish this, is to enable the parents to pay the expense themselves. There are always persons of both sexes to be found in every village, especially when growing into years, capable of such an undertaking. Twenty children, at ten shillings each (and that not more than six months in each year), would be as much as some livings amount to in the remote parts of England; and there are often distressed clergymen's widows to whom such an income would be acceptable. Whatever is given on this account to children answers two purposes: to them it is education, to those who educate them it is a livelihood.—*Author.*

There will then remain one hundred and ten thousand pounds.

Notwithstanding the great modes of relief which the best instituted and best principled government may devise, there will still be a number of smaller cases, which it is good policy as well as beneficence in a nation to consider.

Were twenty shillings to be given to every woman immediately on the birth of a child, who should make the demand, and none will make it whose circumstances do not require it, it might relieve a great deal of instant distress.

There are about two hundred thousand births yearly in England; and if claimed by one-fourth,

The amount would be - - - - - £50,000

And twenty shillings to every new married couple who should claim in like manner. This would not exceed the sum of - - - - - - - £20,000

Also twenty thousand pounds to be appropriated to defray the funeral expenses of persons, who, traveling for work, may die at a distance from their friends. By relieving parishes from this charge, the sick stranger will be better treated.

I shall finish this part of my subject with a plan adapted to the particular condition of a metropolis, such as London.

Cases are continually occurring in a metropolis different from those which occur in the country, and for which a different, or rather an additional mode of relief is necessary. In the country, even in large towns, people have a knowledge of each other and distress never rises to that extreme height it sometimes does in a metropolis. There is no such thing in the country as persons, in the literal sense of the word, starved to death, or dying with cold from the want of a lodging. Yet such cases, and others equally as miserable, happen in London.

Many a youth comes up to London full of expectations, and little or no money, and unless he gets employment he is already half undone; and boys bred up in London without any means of a livelihood, and, as it often happens, of dissolute parents, are in a still worse condition, and servants long out of place are not much better off. In short, a world of little cases is continually arising, which busy or affluent life knows not of, to open the first door to distress. Hunger is not among the postponable wants, and a day, even a few hours, in such a condition, is often the crisis of a life of ruin.

These circumstances, which are the general cause of the little thefts and pilferings that lead to greater, may be prevented. There yet remain twenty thousand pounds out of the four millions of surplus taxes, which, with another fund hereafter to be mentioned, amounting to about twenty thousand pounds more, cannot be better applied than to this purpose. The plan then will be:

First, To erect two or more buildings, or take some already erected, capable of containing at least six thousand persons, and to have in each of these places as many kinds of employment as can be contrived, so that every person who shall come, may find something which he or she can do.

Secondly, To receive all who shall come, without inquiring who or what they are. The only condition to be, that for so much or so many hours work, each person shall receive so many meals of wholesome food, and a warm lodging, at least as good as a barrack. That a certain portion of what each person's work shall be worth shall be reserved, and given to him, or her, on their going away; and that each person shall stay as long, or as short time, or come as often as he chooses, on these conditions.

If each person staid three months, it would assist by rotation twenty-four thousand persons annually, though the real number, at all times, would be but six thousand. By establishing an asylum of this kind, such persons, to whom temporary distresses occur, would have an opportunity to recruit themselves, and be enabled to look out for better employment.

Allowing that their labor paid but one-half the expense of supporting them, after reserving a portion of their earnings for themselves, the sum of forty thousand pounds additional would defray all other charges for even a greater number than six thousand.

The fund properly convertible to this purpose, in addition to the twenty thousand pounds, remaining of the former fund, will be the produce of the tax upon coals, and so iniquitously and wantonly applied to the support of the Duke of Richmond. It is horrid that any man, more especially at the price coals now are, should live on the distresses of a community; and any government permitting such an abuse deserves to be dissolved. This fund is said to be about twenty thousand pounds per annum.

I shall now conclude this plan with enumerating the several particulars, and then proceed to other matters.

The enumeration is as follows:

First,   Abolition of two millions poor-rates.

Secondly,   Provision for two hundred and fifty-two thousand poor families.

Thirdly,   Education for one million and thirty thousand children.

Fourthly, Comfortable provision for one hundred and forty thousand aged persons.

Fifthly, Donation of twenty shillings each for fifty thousand births.

Sixthly, Donation of twenty shillings each for twenty thousand marriages.

Seventhly, Allowance of twenty thousand pounds for the funeral expenses of persons traveling for work, and dying at a distance from their friends.

Eighthly, Employment, at all times, for the casual poor in the cities of London and Westminster.

By the operation of this plan, the poor laws, those instruments of civil torture, will be superseded, and the wasteful expense of litigation prevented. The hearts of the humane will not be shocked by ragged and hungry children, and persons of seventy and eighty years of age begging for bread. The dying poor will not be dragged from place to place to breathe their last, as a reprisal of parish upon parish.

Widows will have maintenance for their children, and will not be carted away, on the death of their husbands, like culprits and criminals; and children will no longer be considered as increasing the distress of their parents. The haunts of the wretched will be known, because it will be to their advantage; and the number of petty crimes, the offspring of distress and poverty, will be lessened. The poor, as well as the rich, will then be interested in the support of government, and the cause and apprehension of riots and tumults will cease.

Ye who sit in ease, and solace yourselves in plenty, and such there are in Turkey and Russia, as well as in England, and who say to yourselves, "Are we not well off," have ye thought of these things? When ye do, ye will cease to speak and feel for yourselves alone.

The plan is easy of practise. It does not embarrass trade by a sudden interruption in the order of taxes, but effects the relief by changing the application of them; and the money necessary for the purpose can be drawn from the excise collections, which are made eight times a year in every market town in England.

Having now arranged and concluded this subject, I proceed to the next.

Taking the present current expenses at seven millions and a half, which is the least amount they are now at, there will remain (after the sum of one million and a half be taken for the new current expenses, and four millions for the before mentioned service) the sum of two millions, part of which to be applied as follows:

Though fleets and armies, by an alliance with France, will, in a great measure, become useless, yet the persons who have devoted themselves to those services, and have thereby unfitted themselves for other lines of life, are not to be sufferers by the means that make others happy. They are a different description of men to those who form or hang about a court.

A part of the army will remain at least for some years, and also of the navy, for which a provision is already made, in the former part of this plan, of one million, which is almost half a million more than the peace establishment of the army and navy in the prodigal times of Charles II.

Suppose, then, fifteen thousand soldiers to be disbanded, and to allow to each of those men three shillings a week during life, clear of all deductions, to be paid in the same manner as the Chelsea college pensioners are paid, and for them to return to their trades and their friends; and also to add fifteen thousand sixpences per week to the pay of the soldiers who shall remain; the annual expense will be:

To the pay of fifteen thousand disbanded soldiers, at
   three shillings per week £117,000
Additional pay to the remaining soldiers 19,500
Suppose the pay to the officers of the disbanded corps
   be of the same amount as the sum allowed to the men 117,000
                                                               £253,500

To prevent bulky estimations, admit the same sum to
  the disbanded navy as to the army, and the same increase of pay 253,500
                                       ————————
                                  Total, £507,000

Every year some part of this sum of half a million
(I omit the odd seven thousand pounds, for the purpose of keeping the account unembarrassed) will fall
in, and the whole of it in time, as it is on the ground
of life annuities, except the increased pay of thirty-
nine thousand pounds. As it falls in, a part of the
taxes may be taken off; for instance, when thirty
thousand pounds fall in, the duty on hops may be
wholly taken off; and as other parts fall in, the duties
on candles and soap may be lessened, till at last they
will totally cease. There now remains at least one
million and a half of surplus taxes.

The tax on houses and windows is one of those
direct taxes, which, like the poor-rates, is not confounded with trade; and when taken off, the relief will
be instantly felt. This tax falls heavy on the middle
class of people.

The amount of this tax by the returns of 1788,
was:

Houses and windows by the act of 1766 . . £385,459 11 7
Houses and windows by the act of 1779 . . 130,739 14 5½
                                            ——————————————
                               Total, £516,199 6 0½

If this tax be struck off, there will then remain about one million of surplus taxes, and as it is always proper to keep a sum in reserve, for incidental matters, it may be best not to extend reductions further, in the first instance, but to consider what may be accomplished by other modes of reform.

Among the taxes most heavily felt is the commutation tax. I shall, therefore, offer a plan for its abolition, by substituting another in its place which will effect three objects at once:

First, That of removing the burden to where it can best be borne.

Secondly, Restoring justice among families by distribution of property.

Thirdly, Extirpating the overgrown influence arising from the unnatural law of primogeniture, and which is one of the principal sources of corruption at elections.

The amount of the commutation tax by the returns of 1788, was £771,657

When taxes are proposed, the country is amused by the plausible language of taxing luxuries. One thing is called a luxury at one time, and something else at another; but the real luxury does not consist in the article, but in the means of procuring it, and this is always kept out of sight.

I know not why any plant or herb of the field should be a greater luxury in one country than in another, but an overgrown estate in either is a luxury at all times, and, as such, is the proper object of taxation. It is, therefore, right to take those kind, tax-making gentlemen upon their own word, and argue on the principle themselves have laid down, that of *taxing luxuries*. If they or their champion, Mr. Burke, who, I fear, is growing out of date like the man in armor, can prove that an estate of twenty, thirty, or forty thousand pounds a year is not a luxury, I will give up the argument.

Admitting that any annual sum, say for instance, one thousand pounds, is necessary or sufficient for the support of a family, consequently the second thousand is of the nature of a luxury, the third still more so, and by proceeding on, we shall at last arrive at a sum that may not improperly be called a prohibitable luxury. It would be impolitic to set bounds to property acquired by industry, and therefore it is right to place the prohibition beyond the probable acquisition to which industry can extend; but there ought to be a limit to property, or the accumulation of it by bequest. It should pass in some other line. The richest in every nation have poor relations, and those very often near in consanguinity.

The following table of progressive taxation is constructed on the above principles, and as a substitute for the commutation tax. It will reach the point of prohibition by a regular operation, and thereby supersede the aristocratical law of primogeniture.

TABLE I

A tax on all estates of the clear yearly value of fifty pounds, after deducting the land tax, and up.

To £500	0s 3d	per pound.
From 500 to 1000	0 6	
On the second thousand	0 9	
On the third ditto	1 0	
On the fourth ditto	1 6	
On the fifth ditto	2 0	
On the sixth ditto	3 0	
On the seventh ditto.	4 0	
On the eighth ditto	5 0	
On the ninth ditto	6 0	
On the tenth ditto	7 0	
On the eleventh ditto	8 0	
On the twelfth ditto	9 0	
On the thirteenth ditto	10 0	
On the fourteenth ditto	11 0	
On the fifteenth ditto	12 0	
On the sixteenth ditto	13 0	
On the seventeenth ditto	14 0	
On the eighteenth ditto	15 0	
On the nineteenth ditto	16 0	
On the twentieth ditto	17 0	
On the twenty-first ditto	18 0	
On the twenty-second ditto	19 0	
On the twenty-third ditto	20 0	

The foregoing table shows the progression per pound on every progressive thousand. The following table shows the amount of the tax on every thousand separately, and in the last column, the total amount of all the separate sums collected.

TABLE II

An estate of £50 per an. at 3d per pound pays £0 12 6

100	"	"	3	"	"	"	1 5	0
200	"	"	3	"	"	"	2 10	0
300	"	"	3	"	"	"	3 15	0
400	"	"	3	"	"	"	5 0	0
500	"	"	3	"	"	"	7 5	0

After £500—the tax of sixpence per pound takes place on the second £500,—consequently an estate of £1000 per annum pays £21 15 and so on.

For the 1st £500 at	0s	3d per pound	£7	5	} £21 15		
2d 500 at	0	6 " "	14	10			
2d 1000 at	0	9 " "	37	10	59	5	
3d 1000 at	1	0 " "	50	0	109	5	
4th 1000 at	1	6 " "	75	0	184	5	
5th 1000 at	2	0 " "	100	0	284	5	
6th 1000 at	3	0 " "	150	0	434	5	
7th 1000 at	4	0 " "	200	0	634	5	
8th 1000 at	5	0 " "	250	0	880	5	
9th 1000 at	6	0 " "	300	0	1180	5	
10th 1000 at	7	0 " "	350	0	1530	5	
11th 1000 at	8	0 " "	400	0	1930	5	
12th 1000 at	9	0 " "	450	0	2380	5	
13th 1000 at	10	0 " "	500	0	2880	5	

For the 14th 1000 at 11s 0d per pound £550 0 £3430 5
   15th 1000 at 12 0 "   "   600 0 4030 5
   16th 1000 at 13 0 "   "   650 0 4680 5
   17th 1000 at 14 0 "   "   700 0 5380 5
   18th 1000 at 15 0 "   "   750 0 6130 5
   19th 1000 at 16 0 "   "   800 0 6930 5
   20th 1000 at 17 0 "   "   850 0 7780 5
   21st 1000 at 18 0 "   "   900 0 8680 5
   22d 1000 at 19 0 "   "   950 0 9630 5
   23d 1000 at 20 0 "   " 1000 0 10630 5

At the twenty-third thousand the tax becomes twenty shillings in the pound, and, consequently, every thousand beyond that sum, can produce no profit but by dividing the estate. Yet, formidable as this tax appears, it will not, I believe, produce so much as the commutation tax; should it produce more, it ought to be lowered to that amount upon estates under two or three thousand a year.

On small and middling estates it is lighter (as it is intended to be) than the commutation tax. It is not till after seven or eight thousand a year that it begins to be heavy. The object is not so much the produce of the tax as the justice of the measure. The aristocracy has screened itself too much, and this serves to restore a part of the lost equilibrium.

As an instance of screening itself, it is only necessary to look back to the first establishment of the excise laws, at what is called the Revolution, or the coming of Charles II. The aristocratical interest then in power, commuted the feudal services itself was under, by laying a tax on beer brewed for *sale*; that is, they compounded with Charles for an exemption from those services for themselves and their heirs, by a tax to be paid by other people. The aristocracy do not purchase beer brewed for sale, but brew their own beer free of the duty, and if any commutation at that time was necessary, it ought to have been at the expense of those for whom the exemptions from those services were intended; * instead of which, it was thrown on an entire different class of men.

But the chief object of this progressive tax (besides the justice of rendering taxes more equal than they are) is, as already stated, to extirpate the overgrown influence arising from the unnatural law of primogeniture, and which is one of the principal sources of corruption at elections.

It would be attended with no good consequences to inquire how such vast estates as thirty, forty, or fifty thousand a year could commence, and that at a time

---

* The tax on beer brewed for sale, from which the aristocracy are exempt, is almost one million more than the present commutation tax, being by the returns of 1788, £1,666,152, and consequently they ought to take on themselves the amount of the commutation tax, as they are already exempted from one which is almost a million greater.—*Author.*

when commerce and manufactures were not in a state to admit of such acquisitions. Let it be sufficient to remedy the evil by putting them in a condition of descending again to the community by the quiet means of apportioning them among all the heirs and heiresses of those families. This will be the more necessary, because hitherto the aristocracy have quartered their younger children and connections upon the public, in useless posts, places and offices, which, when abolished, will leave them destitute, unless the law of primogeniture be also abolished or superseded.

A progressive tax will, in a great measure, effect this object, and that as a matter of interest to the parties most immediately concerned, as will be seen by the following table; which shows the net produce upon every estate, after subtracting the tax.

By this it will appear, that after an estate exceeds thirteen or fourteen thousand a year, the remainder produces but little profit to the holder, and consequently, will either pass to the younger children or to other kindred.

TABLE III

Showing the net produce of every estate from one thousand to twenty-three thousand pounds a year.

No. of thousands per annum.	Total tax subtracted.	Net produce.
£1000	£21	£979
2000	59	1941
3000	109	2891
4000	184	3816
5000	284	4716
6000	434	5566
7000	634	6366
8000	880	7120
9000	1180	7820
10,000	1530	8480
11,000	1930	9070
12,000	2380	9620
13,000	2880	10,120
14,000	3430	10,670
15,000	4030	10,970
16,000	4680	11,320
17,000	5380	11,620
18,000	6130	11,870
19,000	6930	12,170
20,000	7780	12,220
21,000	8680	12,320
22,000	9630	12,370
23,000	10,630	12,370

N.B.   The odd shillings are dropped in this table.

According to this table, an estate cannot produce more than £12,370 clear of the land tax and the progressive tax, and therefore the dividing such estates will follow as a matter of family interest. An estate of £23,000 a year, divided into five estates of four thousand each and one of three, will be charged only £1,129, which is but five per cent, but if held by any one possessor, will be charged £10,630.

Although an inquiry into the origin of those estates be unnecessary, the continuation of them in their present state is another subject. It is a matter of national concern. As hereditary estates, the law has created the evil, and it ought also to provide the remedy. Primogeniture ought to be abolished, not only because it is unnatural and unjust, but because the country suffers by its operation.

By cutting off (as before observed) the younger children from their proper portion of inheritance, the public is loaded with the expense of maintaining them; and the freedom of elections violated by the overbearing influence which this unjust monopoly of family property produces. Nor is this all. It occasions a waste of national property. A considerable part of the land of the country is rendered unproductive, by the great extent of parks and chases which this law serves to keep up, and this at a time when the annual production of grain is not equal to the national consumption.

In short the evils of the aristocratical system are so great and numerous, and so inconsistent with every thing that is just, wise, natural, and beneficent, that when they are considered, there ought not to be a doubt that many, who are now classed under that description, will wish to see such a system abolished.

What pleasure can they derive from contemplating the exposed condition and almost certain beggary of their younger offspring? Every aristocratical family has an appendage of family beggars hanging round it, which, in a few ages, or a few generations, are shook off, and console themselves with telling their tale in almshouses, work-houses and prisons. This is the natural consequence of aristocracy. The peer and the beggar are often of the same family. One extreme produces the other; to make one rich many must be made poor; neither can the system be supported by other means.

There are two classes of people to whom the laws of England are particularly hostile, and those the most helpless: younger children and the poor. Of the former I have just spoken; of the latter I shall mention one instance out of the many that might be produced, and with which I shall close this subject.

Several laws are in existence for regulating and limiting workmen's wages. Why not leave them as free to make their own bargains, as the law-makers are to let their farms and houses? Personal labor is all the property they have. Why is that little, and the little freedom they enjoy, to be infringed? But the injustice will appear stronger, if we consider the operation and effect of such laws. When wages are fixed by what is called a law, the legal wages remain stationary, while every thing else is in progression; and as those who make that law, still continue to lay on new taxes by other laws, they increase the expense of living by one law, and take away the means by another.

But if these gentlemen law-makers and tax-makers thought it right to limit the poor pittance which personal labor can produce, and on which a whole family is to be supported, they certainly must feel themselves happily indulged in a limitation on their own part, of not less than twelve thousand a year, and that of property they never acquired (nor probably any of their ancestors), and of which they have made so ill a use.

Having now finished this subject, I shall bring the several particulars into one view, and then proceed to other matters.

The first eight articles are brought forward from p. 64.

1. Abolition of two millions poor-rates.

2. Provision for two hundred and fifty-two thousand poor families, at the rate of four pounds per head for each child under fourteen years of age; which,

with the addition of two hundred and fifty thousand pounds, provides also education for one million and thirty thousand children.

3.   Annuity of six pounds per annum each for all poor persons, decayed tradesmen, and others, supposed seventy thousand, of the age of fifty years and until sixty.

4.   Annuity of ten pounds each for life for all poor persons, decayed tradesmen and others, supposed seventy thousand, of the age of sixty years.

5.   Donation of twenty shillings each for fifty thousand births.

6.   Donation of twenty shillings each for twenty thousand marriages.

7. . Allowance of twenty thousand pounds for the funeral expenses of persons traveling for work, and dying at a distance from their friends.

8.   Employment at all times for the casual poor in the cities of London and Westminster.

Second enumeration.

9.   Abolition of the tax on houses and windows.

10.   Allowance of three shillings per week for life to fifteen thousand disbanded soldiers, and a proportionate allowance to the officers of the disbanded corps.

11. Increase of pay to the remaining soldiers of £19,500 annually.

12. The same allowance to the disbanded navy, and the same increase of pay, as to the army.

13. Abolition of the commutation tax.

14. Plan of a progressive tax, operating to extirpate the unjust and unnatural law of primogeniture, and the vicious influence of the aristocratical system.*

---

* When inquiries are made into the condition of the poor, various degrees of distress will most probably be found, to render a different arrangement preferable to that which is already proposed. Widows with families will be in greater want than where there are husbands living. There is also a difference in the expense of living in different countries; and more so in fuel.

Suppose fifty thousand extraordinary cases at the rate of ten pounds per family per annum . . .	£500,000
100,000 families, at £8 per family per annum . .	800,000
100,000 families, at 7 " " . . .	700,000
104,000 families, at 5 " " . . .	520,000
And instead of ten shillings per head for the education of other children, to allow fifty shillings per family for that purpose to 50,000 families . . .	250,000
	2,770,000
140,000 aged persons as before	1,120,000
	£3,890,000

The arrangement amounts to the same sum as stated in p. 59, including the £250,000 for education; but it provides (including the aged people) for four hundred and four thousand families, which is almost one-third of all families in England.—*Author.*

There yet remains, as already stated, one million of surplus taxes. Some part of this will be required for circumstances that do not immediately present themselves, and such part as shall not be wanted, will admit of a further reduction of taxes equal to that amount.

Among the claims that justice requires to be made, the condition of the inferior revenue-officers will merit attention. It is a reproach to any government to waste such an immensity of revenue in sinecures and nominal and unnecessary places and offices, and not allow even a decent livelihood to those on whom the labor falls. The salary of the inferior officers of the revenue has stood at the petty pittance of less than fifty pounds a year, for upwards of one hundred years. It ought to be seventy. About one hundred and twenty thousand pounds applied to this purpose, will put all those salaries in a decent condition.

This was proposed to be done almost twenty years ago, but the Treasury Board then in being, startled at it, as it might lead to similar expectations from the army and navy; and the event was, that the King, or somebody for him, applied to Parliament to have his own salary raised a hundred thousand pounds a year, which being done, every thing else was laid aside.

With respect to another class of men, the inferior clergy, I forbear to enlarge on their condition; but all partialities and prejudices for, or against, different modes and forms of religion aside, common justice will determine, whether there ought to be an income of twenty or thirty pounds a year to one man, and of ten thousand to another. I speak on this subject with the more freedom, because I am known not to be a Presbyterian; and therefore the cant cry of court sycophants, about church and meeting, kept up to amuse and bewilder the nation, cannot be raised against me.

Ye simple men on both sides the question, do you not see through this courtly craft? If ye can be kept disputing and wrangling about church and meeting, ye just answer the purpose of every courtier, who lives the while on the spoil of the taxes, and laughs at your credulity. Every religion is good that teaches man to be good; and I know of none that instructs him to be bad.

All the before-mentioned calculations suppose only sixteen millions and a half of taxes paid into the exchequer, after the expense of collection and drawbacks at the custom-house and excise-office are deducted; whereas the sum paid into the exchequer, is very nearly, if not quite, seventeen millions. The taxes raised in Scotland and Ireland are expended in those countries, and therefore their savings will come out of their own taxes; but if any part be paid into the English exchequer, it might be remitted. This will not make one hundred thousand pounds a year difference.

There now remains only the national debt to be considered. In the year 1789, the interest, exclusive of the tontine, was £9,150,138. How much the capital has been reduced since that time the Minister best knows. But after paying the interest, abolishing the tax on houses and windows, the commutation tax and the poor-rates, and making all the provisions for the poor, for the education of children, the support of the aged, the disbanded part of the army and navy, and increasing the pay of the remainder, there will be a surplus of one million.

The present scheme of paying off the national debt appears to me, speaking as an indifferent person, to be an ill concerted, if not a fallacious job. The burden of the national debt consists not in its being so many millions, or so many hundred millions, but in the quantity of taxes collected every year to pay the interest. If this quantity continues the same, the burden of the national debt is the same to all intents and purposes, be the capital more or less.

The only knowledge the public can have of the reduction of the debt, must be through the reduction, of taxes for paying the interest. The debt, therefore, is not reduced one farthing to the public by all the millions that have been paid; and it would require more money now to purchase up the capital, than when the scheme began.

Digressing for a moment at this point, to which I shall return again, I look back to the appointment of Mr. Pitt as Minister.

I was then in America. The war was over; and though resentment had ceased, memory was still alive.

When the news of the coalition arrived, though it was a matter of no concern to me as a citizen of America, I felt it as a man. It had something in it which shocked, by publicly sporting with decency, if not with principle. It was impudence in Lord North; it was a want of firmness in Mr. Fox.

Mr. Pitt was, at that time, what may be called a maiden character in politics. So far from being hackneyed, he appeared not to be initiated into the first mysteries of court intrigue. Every thing was in his favor. Resentment against the coalition served as friendship to him, and his ignorance of vice was credited for virtue. With the return of peace, com-

merce and prosperity would rise of itself; yet even
this increase was thrown to his account.

When he came to the helm, the storm was over, and
he had nothing to interrupt his course. It required
even ingenuity to be wrong, and he succeeded. A
little time showed him the same sort of man as his
predecessors had been. Instead of profiting by those
errors which had accumulated a burden of taxes un-
paralleled in the world, he sought, I might almost say,
he advertised for enemies, and provoked means to
increase taxation. Aiming at something, he knew not
what, he ransacked Europe and India for adventures,
and abandoning the fair pretensions he began with,
became the knight-errant of modern times.

It is unpleasant to see a character throw itself
away. It is more so to see one's self deceived. Mr.
Pitt had merited nothing, but he promised much. He
gave symptoms of a mind superior to the meanness
and corruption of courts. His apparent candor encouraged expectations; and the public confidence,
stunned, wearied, and confounded by a chaos of parties, revived and attached itself to him. But mistak-
ing, as he has done, the disgust of the nation against
the coalition, for merit in himself, he has rushed into
measures, which a man less supported would not have
presumed to act.

All this seems to show that change of ministers amounts to nothing. One goes out, another comes in, and still the same measures, vices, and extravagance are pursued. It signifies not who is minister. The defect lies in the system. The foundation and super-structure of the government is bad. Prop it as you please, it continually sinks into court government, and ever will.

I return, as I promised, to the subject of the national debt, that offspring of the Dutch-Anglo Revolution, and its handmaid, the Hanover Succession.

But it is now too late to inquire how it began. Those to whom it is due have advanced the money; and whether it was well or ill spent, or pocketed, is not their crime. It is, however, easy to see, that as the nation proceeds in contemplating the nature and principles of government, and to understand taxes, and make comparisons between those of America, France, and England, it will be next to impossible to keep it in the same torpid state it has hitherto been. Some reform must, from the necessity of the case, soon begin. It is not whether these principles press with little or much force in the present moment. They are out. They are abroad in the world, and no force can stop them. Like a secret told, they are beyond recall; and he must be blind indeed that does not see that a change is already beginning.

Nine millions of dead taxes is a serious thing; and this not only for bad, but in a great measure for foreign government. By putting the power of making war into the hands of foreigners who came for what they could get, little else was to be expected than what has happened.

Reasons are already advanced in this work, showing that whatever the reforms in the taxes may be, they ought to be made in the current expenses of government, and not in the part applied to the interest of the national debt. By remitting the taxes of the poor, *they* will be totally relieved and all discontent will be taken away; and by striking off such of the taxes as are already mentioned, the nation will more than recover the whole expense of the mad American War.

There will then remain only the national debt as a subject of discontent, and in order to remove, or rather prevent this, it would be good policy in the stockholders themselves to consider it as property, subject like all other property, to bear some portion of the taxes. It would give to it both popularity and security, and, as a great part of its present inconvenience is balanced by the capital which it keeps alive, a measure of this kind would so far add to that balance as to silence objections.

This may be done by such gradual means as to accomplish all that is necessary with the greatest ease and convenience.

Instead of taxing the capital, the best method would be to tax the interest by some progressive ratio, and to lessen the public taxes in the same proportion as the interest diminished.

Suppose the interest was taxed one half-penny in the pound the first year, a penny more the second, and to proceed by a certain ratio to be determined upon, always less than any other tax upon property. Such a tax would be subtracted from the interest at the time of payment, without any expense of collection.

One halfpenny in the pound would lessen the interest and consequently the taxes, twenty thousand pounds. The tax on wagons amounts to this sum, and this tax might be taken off the first year. The second year the tax on female servants, or some other of the like amount, might also be taken off, and by proceeding in this manner, always applying the tax raised from the property of the debt towards its extinction, and not carrying it to the current services, it would liberate itself.

The stockholders, notwithstanding this tax, would pay less taxes than they do now. What they would save by the extinction of the poor-rates and the tax on houses and windows, and the commutation tax, would be considerably greater than what this tax, slow, but certain in its operation, amounts to.

It appears to me to be prudence to look out for measures that may apply under any circumstances that may approach. There is, at this moment, a crisis in the affairs of Europe that requires it. Preparation now is wisdom. If taxation be once let loose, it will be difficult to reinstate it; neither would the relief be so effectual, as if it proceeded by some certain and gradual reduction.

The fraud, hypocrisy, and imposition of governments are now beginning to be too well understood to promise them any longer career. The farce of monarchy and aristocracy, in all countries, is following that of chivalry, and Mr. Burke is dressing for the funeral. Let it then pass quietly to the tomb of all other follies, and the mourners be comforted.

The time is not very distant, when England will laugh at itself for sending to Holland, Hanover, Zell, or Brunswick for men, at the expense of a million a year, who understood neither her laws, her language, nor her interest, and whose capacities would scarcely

have fitted them for the office of a parish constable.
If government could be trusted to such hands, it must
be some easy and simple thing indeed, and materials
fit for all the purposes may be found in every town
and village in England.

When it shall be said in any country in the world,
"My poor are happy; neither ignorance nor distress is
to be found among them; my jails are empty of pris-
oners, my streets of beggars; the aged are not in
want, the taxes are not oppressive; the rational world
is my friend, because I am a friend of its happiness:"
—when these things can be said, then may that country boast of its constitution and its government.
Within the space of a few years we have seen two
revolutions, those of America and France. In the
former, the contest was long and the conflict severe;
in the latter, the nation acted with such a consolidated
impulse, that having no foreign enemy to contend
with, the revolution was complete in power the moment it appeared.

From both those instances it is evident, that the
greatest forces that can be brought into the field of
revolutions, are reason and common interest. Where
these can have the opportunity of acting, opposition
dies with fear, or crumbles away by conviction. It is
a great standing which they have now universally

obtained; and we may hereafter hope to see revolutions, or changes in governments, produced with the same quiet operation by which any measure, determinable by reason and discussion, is accomplished.

When a nation changes its opinion and habits of thinking, it is no longer to be governed as before; but it would not only be wrong, but bad policy, to attempt by force what ought to be accomplished by reason. Rebellion consists in forcibly opposing the general will of a nation, whether by a party or by a government. There ought, therefore, to be in every nation a method of occasionally ascertaining the state of public opinion with respect to government.

On this point the old Government of France was superior to the present Government of England, because, on extraordinary occasions, recourse could be had to what was then called the States-General. But in England there are no such occasional bodies; and as to those who are now called representatives, a great part of them are mere machines of the court, placemen and dependents.

I presume, that though all the people of England pay taxes, not a hundredth part of them are electors, and the members of one of the Houses of Parliament represent nobody but themselves. There is, therefore, no power but the voluntary will of the people that has a right to act in any matter respecting a general reform; and by the same right that two persons can confer on such a subject, a thousand may. The object, in all such preliminary proceedings, is to find out what the general sense of a nation is, and to be governed by it.

If it prefer a bad or defective government to a reform, or choose to pay ten times more taxes than there is any occasion for, it has a right to do so; and so long as the majority do not impose conditions on the minority, different from what they impose upon themselves, though there may be much error, there is no injustice. Neither will the error continue long. Reason and discussion will soon bring things right, however wrong they may begin.

By such a process no tumult is to be apprehended. The poor in all countries are naturally both peaceable and grateful in all reforms in which their interest and happiness are included. It is only by neglecting and rejecting them that they become tumultuous.

The objects that now press on the public attention are the French Revolution, and the prospect of a general revolution in governments. Of all nations in Europe, there is none so much interested in the French Revolution as England. Enemies for ages, and that at a vast expense, and without any national object, the opportunity now presents itself or amicably closing the scene, and joining their efforts to reform the rest of Europe.

By doing this, they will not only prevent the further effusion of blood, and increase of taxes, but be in a condition of getting rid of a considerable part of their present burdens, as has been already stated. Long experience, however, has shown that reforms of this kind are not those which old governments wish to promote, and therefore, it is to nations, and not to such governments, that these matters present themselves.

In the preceding part of this work I have spoken of an alliance between England, France and America, for purposes that were to be afterwards mentioned. Though I have no direct authority on the part of America, I have good reason to conclude, that she is disposed to enter into a consideration of such a measure, provided that the governments with which she might ally, acted as national governments and not as courts enveloped in intrigue and mystery.

That France as a nation and a national government would prefer an alliance with England, is a matter of certainty. Nations, like individuals, who have long been enemies, without knowing each other, or knowing why, become better friends when they discover the errors and impositions under which they had acted.

Admitting, therefore, the probability of such a connection, I will state some matters by which such an alliance, together with that of Holland, might render service, not only to the parties immediately concerned, but to all parts of Europe.

It is, I think, quite certain, that if the fleets of England, France and Holland were confederated, they could propose, with effect, a limitation to, and a general dismantling of, all the navies in Europe, to a certain proportion to be agreed upon.

First, That no new ship of war shall be built by any power in Europe, themselves included.

Secondly, That all the navies now in existence shall be put back, suppose to one-tenth of their present force. This will save to France and England at least two millions annually to each, and their relative force be in the same proportion as it is now. If men will permit themselves to think, as rational beings ought to think, nothing can appear more ridiculous and absurd, exclusive of all moral reflections, than to be at the expense of building navies, filling them with men, and then hauling them into the ocean, to try which can sink each other fastest.

Peace, which costs nothing, is attended with infinitely more advantage than any victory with all its expense. But this, though it best answers the purpose of nations, does not that of court governments, whose habitual policy is pretense for taxation, places and offices.

It is, I think, also certain, that the above confederated powers, together with that of the United States of America, can propose, with effect, to Spain, the independence of South America, and the opening those countries, of immense extent and wealth, to the general commerce of the world, as North America now is.

With how much more glory and advantage to itself does a nation act, when it exerts its powers to rescue the world from bondage, and to create to itself friends, than when it employs those powers to increase ruin, desolation and misery. The horrid scene that is now acting by the English Government in the East Indies, is fit only to be told of Goths and Vandals, who, destitute of principle, robbed and tortured the world which they were incapable of enjoying.

The opening of South America would produce an immense field for commerce, and a ready money market for manufactures, which the Eastern world does not. The East is already a country of manufactures, the importation of which is not only an injury to the manufactures of England, but a drain upon its specie. The balance against England by this trade is regularly upward of half a million annually sent out in the East India ships, in silver; and this is the reason, together with German intrigue, and German subsidies, that there is so little silver in England.

But any war is harvest to such governments, however ruinous it may be to a nation. It serves to keep up deceitful expectations, which prevent people from looking into the defects and abuses of government. It is the *lo here!* and the *lo there!* that amuses and cheats the multitude.

Never did so great an opportunity offer itself to England, and to all Europe, as is produced by the two revolutions of America and France. By the former, freedom has a national champion in the Western world; and by the latter, in Europe. When another nation shall join France, despotism and bad government will scarcely dare to appear. To use a trite expression, the iron is becoming hot all over Europe. The insulted German and the enslaved Spaniard, the Russ and the Pole are beginning to think. The present age will hereafter merit to be called the Age of Reason, and the present generation will appear to the future as the Adam of a new world.

When all the governments of Europe shall be established on the representative system, nations will become acquainted, and the animosities and prejudices fomented by the intrigues and artifice of courts will cease. The oppressed soldier will become a free man; and the tortured sailor, no longer dragged through the streets like a felon, will pursue his mercantile voyage in safety. It would be better that nations should continue the pay of their soldiers during their lives, and give them their discharge and restore them to freedom and their friends, and cease recruiting, than retain such multitudes at the same expense, in a condition useless to society and to themselves.

As soldiers have hitherto been treated in most countries, they might be said to be without a friend. Shunned by the citizen on an apprehension of their being enemies to liberty, and too often insulted by those who commanded them, their condition was a double oppression. But where genuine principles of liberty pervade a people, everything is restored to order; and the soldier civilly treated, returns the civility.

In contemplating revolutions, it is easy to perceive that they may arise from two distinct causes; the one, to avoid or get rid of some calamity, the other, to obtain some great and positive good; and the two may be distinguished by the names of active and passive revolutions. In those which proceed from the former cause, the temper becomes incensed and soured; and the redress, obtained by danger, is too often sullied by revenge.

But in those which proceed from the latter, the heart, rather animated than agitated, enters serenely upon the subject. Reason and discussion, persuasion and conviction, become the weapons in the contest, and it is only when those are attempted to be suppressed that recourse is had to violence.

When men unite in agreeing that a *thing is good,* could it be obtained, such as relief from a burden of taxes and the extinction of corruption, the object is more than half accomplished. What they approve as the end, they will promote in the means.

Will any man say in the present excess of taxation, falling so heavily on the poor, that a remission of five pounds annually of taxes to one hundred and four thousand poor families is not a *good thing?* Will he say that a remission of seven pounds annually to one hundred thousand other poor families; of eight pounds annually to another hundred thousand poor families, and of ten pounds annually to fifty thousand poor and widowed families, are not *good things?*

And, to proceed a step further in this climax, will he say, that to provide against the misfortunes to which all human life is subject, by securing six pounds annually for all poor, distressed, and reduced persons of the age of fifty and until sixty, and of ten pounds annually after sixty, is not a *good thing?*

Will he say that an abolition of two millions of poor-rates to the housekeepers, and of the whole of the house and window-light tax and of the commutation tax, is not a *good thing?* Or will he say, that to abolish corruption is a *bad thing?*

If, therefore, the good to be obtained be worthy of a passive, rational and costless revolution, it would be bad policy to prefer waiting for a calamity that should force a violent one. I have no idea, considering the reforms which are now passing and spreading throughout Europe, that England will permit herself to be the last; and where the occasion and the opportunity quietly offer, it is better than to wait for a turbulent necessity. It may be considered as an honor to the animal faculties of man to obtain redress by courage and danger, but it is far greater honor to the rational faculties to accomplish the same object by reason, accommodation, and general consent.*

---

* I know it is the opinion of many of the most enlightened characters in France (there always will be those who see further

As reforms, or revolutions, call them which you please, extend themselves among nations, those nations will form connections and conventions, and when a few are thus confederated, the progress will be rapid, till despotism and corrupt government be totally expelled, at least out of two quarters of the world, Europe and America. The Algerine piracy may then be commanded to cease, for it is only by the malicious policy of old governments against each other that it exists.

Throughout this work, various and numerous as the subjects are, which I have taken up and investi-

---

into events than others), not only among the general mass of citizens, but of many of the principal members of the former National Assembly, that the monarchical plan will not continue many years in that country. They have found out, that, as wisdom cannot be made hereditary, power ought not; and that for a man to merit a million sterling a year from a nation, he ought to have a mind capable of comprehending from an atom to a universe, which, if he had, he would be above receiving the pay.

But they wished not to appear to lead the nation faster than its own reason and interest dictated. In all the conversations where I have been present upon this subject, the idea always was, that when such a time, from the general opinion of the nation, shall arrive, that the honorable and liberal method would be, to make a handsome present in fee simple to the person, whoever he may be, that shall then be in the monarchical office, and for him to retire to the enjoyment of private life, possessing his share of general rights and privileges, and to be no more accountable to the public for his time and his conduct than any other citizen.— *Author.*

gated, there is only a single paragraph upon religion, viz. *"that every religion is good that teaches man to be good."*

I have carefully avoided to enlarge upon the subject, because I am inclined to believe that what is called the present Ministry wish to see contentions about religion kept up, to prevent the nation turning its attention to subjects of government. It is as if they were to say, *"look that way, or any way but this."*

But as religion is very improperly made a political machine, and the reality of it is thereby destroyed, I will conclude this work with stating in what light religion appears to me.

If we suppose a large family of children, who, on any particular day, or particular occasion, make it a custom to present to their parents some token of their affection and gratitude, each of them would make a different offering, and most probably in a different manner.

Some would pay their congratulations in themes of verse and prose, by some little devices, as their genius dictated, or according to what they thought would please; and, perhaps, the least of all, not able to do any of those things, would ramble into the garden, or the field, and gather what it thought the prettiest flower it could find, though, perhaps, it might be but a simple weed. The parents would be more gratified by such a variety than if the whole of them had acted on a concerted plan, and each had made exactly the same offering.

This would have the cold appearance of contrivance, or the harsh one of control. But of all unwelcome things, nothing would more afflict the parent than to know that the whole of them had afterwards gotten together by the ears, boys and girls, fighting, reviling, and abusing each other about which was the best or the worst present.

Why may we not suppose that the great Father of all is pleased with variety of devotion; and that the greatest offense we can act is that by which we seek to torment and render each other miserable? For my own part I am fully satisfied that what I am now doing, with an endeavor to conciliate mankind, to render their condition happy, to unite nations that have hitherto been enemies, and to extirpate the horrid practise of war and break the chains of slavery and oppression, is acceptable in His sight, and being the best service I can perform I act it cheerfully.

I do not believe that any two men, on what are called doctrinal points, think alike who think at all. It is only those who have not thought that appear to agree. It is in this case as with what is called the British Constitution; it has been taken for granted to be good, and encomiums have supplied the place of proof. But when the nation comes to examine into its principles and the abuses it admits, it will be found to have more defects than I have pointed out in this work and the former.

As to what are called national religions, we may, with as much propriety, talk of national gods. It is either political craft or the remains of the pagan system, when every nation had its separate and particular deity.

Among all the writers of the English Church clergy, who have treated on the general subject of religion, the present Bishop of Llandaff has not been excelled, and it is with much pleasure that I take this opportunity of expressing this token of respect.

I have now gone through the whole of the subject, at least, as far as it appears to me at present.

It has been my intention for the five years I have been in Europe to offer an address to the people of England on the subject of government, if the opportunity presented itself before I returned to America. Mr. Burke has thrown it in my way, and I thank him. On a certain occasion, three years ago, I pressed him to propose a national convention, to be fairly elected, for the purpose of taking the state of the nation into consideration; but I found that however strongly the parliamentary current was then setting against the party he acted with, their policy was to keep everything within that field of corruption, and trust to accidents. Long experience had shown that parliaments would follow any change of ministers, and on this they rested their hopes and their expectations.

Formerly, when divisions arose respecting governments, recourse was had to the sword, and a civil war ensued. That savage custom is exploded by the new system, and reference is had to national conventions. Discussion and the general will arbitrates the question, and to this private opinion yields with a good grace, and order is preserved uninterrupted.

Some gentlemen have affected to call the principles upon which this work and the former part of the "Rights of Man" are founded "a new fangled doctrine." The question is not whether these principles are new or old, but whether they are right or wrong. Suppose the former, I will show their effect by a figure easily understood.

It is now toward the middle of February. Were I to take a turn into the country, the trees would present a leafless, wintery appearance. As people are apt to pluck twigs as they go along, I perhaps might do the same, and by chance might observe that a *single bud* on that twig has begun to swell. I should reason very unnaturally, or rather not reason at all, to suppose *this* was the *only bud* in England which had this appearance.

Instead of deciding thus, I should instantly conclude that the same appearance was beginning, or about to begin, everywhere; and though the vegetable sleep will continue longer on some trees and plants than on others, and though some of them may not *blossom* for two or three years, all will be in leaf in the summer, except those which are *rotten*. What pace the political summer may keep with the natural, no human foresight can determine. It is, however, not difficult to perceive that the spring is begun.

Thus wishing, as I sincerely do, freedom and happiness to all nations, I close the SECOND PART.

Appendix

AS the publication of this work has been delayed beyond the time intended, I think it not improper, all circumstances considered, to state the causes that have occasioned that delay.

The reader will probably observe that some parts in the plan contained in this work for reducing the taxes, and certain parts in Mr. Pitt's speech at the opening of the present session, Tuesday, January 31, are so much alike, as to induce a belief that either the author had taken the hint from Mr. Pitt, or Mr. Pitt from the author. I will first point out the parts that are similar, and then state such circumstances as I am acquainted with, leaving the reader to make his own conclusion.

Considering it as almost an unprecedented case that taxes should be proposed to be taken off, it is equally extraordinary that such a measure should occur to two persons at the same time; and still more so (considering the vast variety and multiplicity of taxes) that they should hit on the same specific taxes. Mr. Pitt has mentioned, in his speech, the tax on *carts and wagons;* that on *female servants;* the lowering the tax on *candles,* and the taking off the tax of three shillings on *houses* having under seven windows.

Every one of those specific taxes are a part of the plan contained in this work, and proposed also to be taken off. Mr. Pitt's plan, it is true, goes no further than to a reduction of three hundred and twenty thousand pounds; and the reduction proposed in this work, to nearly six millions. I have made my calculations on only sixteen millions and an half of revenue, still asserting that it was very nearly, if not quite, seventeen millions. Mr. Pitt states it at

£16,690,000. I know enough of the matter to say, that he has not *over*stated it. Having thus given the particulars, which correspond in this work and his speech, I will state a chain of circumstances that may lead to some explanation.

The first hint for lessening the taxes, and that as a consequence flowing from the French Revolution, is to be found in the Address and Declaration of the gentlemen who met at the Thatched-House tavern, August 20, 1791. Among many other particulars stated in that address, is the following, put as an interrogation to the government opposers of the French Revolution. *"Are they sorry that the pretense for new oppressive taxes, and the occasion for continuing many old taxes will be at an end?"*

It is well known, that the persons who chiefly frequent the Thatched-House tavern, are men of court connections, and so much did they take this address and declaration respecting the French Revolution and the reduction of taxes, in disgust, that the landlord was under the necessity of informing the gentlemen, who composed the meeting of the 20th of August, and who proposed holding another meeting, that he could not receive them.*

---

* The gentleman who signed the *Address and Declaration* as chairman of the meeting, Mr. Horne Tooke, being generally sup-

What was only hinted at in the *"Address and Declaration"* respecting taxes and principles of government, will be found reduced to a regular system in this work. But as Mr. Pitt's speech contains some of the same things respecting taxes, I now come to give the circumstances before alluded to.

The case is this: This work was intended to be published just before the meeting of Parliament, and for that purpose a considerable part of the copy was put into the printer's hands in September, and all the remaining copy, as far as page 160 [first English edition], which contains the part to which Mr. Pitt's speech is similar, was given to him full six weeks

---

posed to be the person who drew it up, and having spoken much in commendation of it, has been jocularly accused of praising his own work. To free him from this embarrassment, and to save him the repeated trouble of mentioning the author, as he had not failed to do, I make no hesitation in saying, that as the opportunity of benefiting by the French Revolution easily occurred to me, I drew up the publication in question, and showed it to him and some other gentlemen; who, fully approving it, held a meeting for the purpose of making it public, and subscribed to the amount of fifty guineas to defray the expense of advertising.

I believe there are at this time in England a greater number of men acting on disinterested principles and determined to look into the nature and practises of government themselves, and not blindly trust, as has hitherto been the case, either to government generally, or to parliaments, or to parliamentary opposition, than at any former period. Had this been done a century ago, corruption and taxation had not arrived at the height they are now at.—*Author.*

before the meeting of Parliament, and he was informed of the time at which it was to appear. He had composed nearly the whole about a fortnight before the time of Parliament's meeting, and had printed as far as page 112, and had given me a proof of the next sheet, up to page 128.

It was then in sufficient forwardness to be out at the time proposed, as two other sheets were ready for striking off. I had before told him, that if he thought he should be straitened for time, I could get part of the work done at another press, which he desired me not to do. In this manner the work stood on the Tuesday fortnight preceding the meeting of Parliament, when all at once, without any previous intimation, though I had been with him the evening before, he sent me by one of his workmen, all the remaining copy, from page 112, declining to go on with the work *on any consideration.*

To account for this extraordinary conduct I was totally at a loss, as he stopped at the part where the arguments on systems and principles of government closed, and where the plan for the reduction of taxes, the education of children, and the support of the poor and the aged begins; and still more especially, as he had, at the time of his beginning to print, and before he had seen the whole copy, offered a thousand pounds for the copy-right, together with the future copy-right of the former part of the "Rights of Man."

I told the person who brought me this offer that I should not accept it, and wished it not to be renewed, giving him as my reason, that though I believed the printer to be an honest man, I would never put it in the power of any printer or publisher to suppress or alter a work of mine, by making him master of the copy, or give to him the right of selling it to any minister, or to any other person, or to treat as a mere matter of traffic, that which I intended should operate as a principle.

His refusal to complete the work (which he could not purchase) obliged me to seek for another printer, and this of consequence would throw the publication back until after the meeting of Parliament, otherwise it would have appeared that Mr. Pitt had only taken up a part of the plan which I had more fully stated.

Whether that gentleman, or any other, had seen the work or any part of it, is more than I have authority to say. But the manner in which the work was returned, and the particular time at which this was done, and that after the offers he had made, are suspicious circumstances. I know what the opinion of booksellers and publishers is upon such a case, but as to my own opinion, I choose to make no declaration. There are many ways by which proof sheets may be procured by other persons before a work publicly appears; to which I shall add a certain circumstance, which is,

A Ministerial bookseller in Piccadilly who has been employed, as common report says, by a clerk of one of the boards closely connected with the Ministry (the Board of Trade and Plantations, of which Hawksbury is president,) to publish what he calls my life, (I wish his own life and that those of the Cabinet were as good,) used to have his books printed at the same printing office that I employed; but when the former part of the "Rights of Man" came out, he took his work away in a dudgeon; and about a week or ten days before the printer returned my copy, he came to make him an offer of his work again, which was accepted.

This would consequently give him admission into the printing office where the sheets of this work were then lying; and as booksellers and printers are free with each other, he would have the opportunity of seeing what was going on. Be the case, however, as it may, Mr. Pitt's plan, little and diminutive as it is, would have made a very awkward appearance, had this work appeared at the time the printer had engaged to finish it.

I have now stated the particulars which occasioned the delay, from the proposal to purchase, to the refusal to print. If all the gentlemen are innocent, it is very unfortunate for them that such a variety of suspicious circumstances should, without any design, arrange themselves together.

Having now finished this part, I will conclude with stating another circumstance.

About a fortnight or three weeks before the meeting of Parliament, a small addition, amounting to about twelve shillings and sixpence a year, was made to the pay of the soldiers, or rather their pay was docked so much less. Some gentleman who knew in part that this work would contain a plan of reforms respecting the oppressed condition of soldiers, wished me to add a note to the work, signifying that the part upon that subject had been in the printer's hands some weeks before that addition of pay was proposed.

I declined doing this, lest it should be interpreted into an air of vanity, or an endeavor to excite suspicion (for which perhaps there might be no grounds) that some of the Government gentlemen had, by some means or other, made out what this work would contain; and had not the printing been interrupted so

as to occasion a delay beyond the time fixed for publication, nothing contained in this appendix would
have appeared.

Thomas Paine.

MISCELLANEOUS ESSAYS

TO THE AUTHORS OF "LE RÉPUBLICAIN"

THIS letter, dated at Paris, June, 1791, was addressed by Paine to three of his disciples, Messieurs Condorcet, Nicolas de Bonneville and Lanthenas, who, with Achille Duchâtelet, son of a French duke, were planning to publish an anti-royalist organ in the cause of liberty. M. Lanthenas afterwards translated into French the "Rights of Man" and ranks as Paine's best translator into that language.

This group of young Frenchmen led in the formation of a Republican Club, the ideals and principles of which were to be enunciated by "Le Républicain." Only one number of the publication seems to have been issued.

I HAVE been informed by M. Duchâtelet that it is the purpose of certain persons to begin the publication of a work entitled "Le Républicain."

Being the citizen of a land that recognizes no majesty but that of the people, no government except that of its own representatives, and no sovereignty except that of the laws, I tender you my services in helping forward the success of those principles which honor a nation and contribute to the advancement of the entire world; and I tender them not only because my country is bound to yours by the ties of friendship and gratitude, but because I venerate the moral and political character of those who have taken part in the present enterprise, and feel

115

proud of being their associate. Unfortunately all my productions have been composed in English, and can be of slight advantage to the cause, except through the medium of translation, so that, I suppose, the services I would render can never be commensurate with my desires. Moreover, I shall have to spend a portion of this summer in England and Ireland.

The public are generally aware that I subscribe the words COMMON SENSE to whatever I publish, and, therefore, I shall use this pen-name in my contributions to your work, so that no one may commit the error of attributing to me productions in which I have had no share. At the same time, I shall try to render my opinions on the political situation so self-evident that their tendency cannot be mistaken. If such definiteness of expression be always desirable, it is especially necessary in the present circumstance, because we are confronting a situation concerning which there should be no possibility of misunderstanding our ideas. For this reason the title of your publication gives me much satisfaction. The words "The Republican" imply that it is solely concerned about the *Res-publica,* namely, the interests of the state, and that includes all the ideas we should entertain of government in general.

The very word "Monarchy" signifies, in its primary meaning, the *despotic rule of one individual*, though that individual be a madman, a tyrant, or a hypocrite; kings and courtiers have, indeed, succeeded in giving it a gentler meaning but, for all that, the very term is in itself an insult to a people, for it is susceptible of no other significance than that which I have attached to it. In this relation, then, France is not a monarchy, and to style it so is to insult her. The abject servitude which is the concomitant of monarchical government no more exists in France now than it does in America, and therefore she should regard it as a thing to be scorned.

One of the absurd notions which the dishonesty or the ignorance of the supporters of monarchy have scattered through the world is that, while the republican form of government may be suited to a small country, the monarchical is the only one that harmonizes with a large one. But this opinion, though by the agencies of courts it has been spread broadcast through monarchical countries, is in accordance neither with principle nor with experience.

No government can be considered to have completely fulfilled its functions if it is not thoroughly acquainted with all the varied interests and all the different parts of the nation. For this reason it might be said that monarchy is adapted rather to a small country in which the monarch may easily become familiar with the affairs of the entire population. On the other hand, how can a single individual become familiar with the affairs of an extensive territory embracing a multiplicity of diverse interests? His helpless ignorance of matters that affect the people must necessarily lead to the establishment of a tyrannical form of government. As evidence of the truth of this proposition, we have only to point to Spain, Russia, Germany, Turkey and the whole of Asia.—That I may live to see the freedom of these lands is my ardent desire.

In fact, the only system of government that can insure anything like adequate attention to every portion of an extended territory is the government that has its source in popular representation.

Such representation is the most potent and vigorous organ of the opinion of a nation. It acts so powerfully on the minds of citizens that they approve of it even without knowing why. Every part of France, no matter how far away it may be from its center, is aware that that center constitutes France, and that in its center it has its integral being. This is the feeling of the citizen, however remote may be his abode: he knows that his rights are protected, and, if he is a soldier, he is assured that he is not enslaved by a tyrant, but that he is the citizen of a free nation, and, therefore, bound to defend it.

It is true that certain countries, such as Holland, Berne, Genoa, Venice, etc., call themselves Republics; but these countries do not merit such a designation. All the principles upon which they are founded are in direct contradiction to every republican sentiment, and they are really in a condition of absolute servitude to an aristocracy.

During the early period of a revolution mistakes are likely enough to be committed—mistakes in principle or in practise; or perhaps, mistakes both in principle and practise. When men are in the early stage of freedom, they are not all sufficiently instructed to be able to inform one another mutually of their several opinions, and so they become the victims of a sort of timidity that hinders them from reaching at a single bound that elevation which they have the *right* to attain. We have witnessed symptoms of this imperfection at the beginning of the present Revolution. Fortunately, they were manifested before the Constitution was fully established, so that whatever defects were apparent could be corrected.

Hereditary succession is never founded on *right;* consequently, it has no real existence. To sanction such a fallacy is to sanction the fallacy of the right of certain individuals, either now born or about to be born, to the possession of human beings as their property! It is to declare that our posterity is to be classed with the animal creation, destitute alike of will and of right! Such a conception debases human nature and should forever be effaced from the soul of that humanity which it dishonors.

Nay, so opposed to the rights of man is hereditary succession that even if we, instead of our descendants, should at some future period return to life, we should not then have the right to abdicate those rights which would be our own peculiar possession. On what argument, therefore, can we base our claim to rob of their rights children who will one day become men? How is it we are unable to see the wrong we inflict upon our posterity when we attempt to prolong the rule of those infamous despots the continuance of whose vices, and of whose vices alone, we can surely foretell?

Only when the French Constitution conforms to the *Declaration of Rights* can France be justly entitled to be called a *civic empire;* because then only will its government be the empire of laws based upon the grand republican principles of Elective Representation and the Rights of Man. On the other hand,

Rights of Man and Constitution Badge

Preserved at the Musee de Carnavalet, Paris. This badge is reminiscent of Paine, who wrote "Rights of Man" and helped frame for France a republican constitution.

Monarchy and Hereditary succession are totally inconsistent with the very fundamental principles of constitutional government.

I venture to think that the preceding opinions will show you that I am a sound Republican. Indeed, my conviction of the stability of these principles is so firm that I look forward to their triumph in France as well as in America. The pride of human nature will emphasize their truth, contribute to their success and inspire mankind with a feeling of shame at the thought of the very existence of Monarchy.

I remain, Messieurs, with great respect,

Your friend

THOMAS PAINE.

A REPUBLICAN MANIFESTO

THIS Manifesto or Proclamation of a Republic was placarded in Paris on July 1, 1791, after the flight of Louis XVI. Its authorship is ascribed to Paine by Étienne Dumont in his "Recollections of Mirabeau," wherein it is stated that "Paine was its author. Duchâtelet had adopted and was resolved to sign, placard the walls of Paris with it and take the consequences. He wanted me to translate it. I declined, asking if he had consulted Lafayette and other republican leaders. He had not: he and Paine had acted alone—an American and an impulsive nobleman had put themselves forward to change the whole governmental system of France. . . . The placarding of the document was denounced by the Assembly —but some of the seed sown by the audacious hand of Paine were planted and were soon budding in leading minds."

BROTHERS AND FELLOW-CITIZENS: Did we require the most indubitable evidence that the presence of a king is rather a bane than a blessing, that as an element of the political system he is without force or value, and that he is an onerous affliction whose weight crushes the people, we should discover it in the calm attitude of the people during the King's flight, and the air of unconcern with which they have viewed his reappearance.

Do not allow fallacies to delude you; the whole question may be resolved into four simple propositions:

His flight is equivalent to abdication; for, in abandoning his throne, he has abandoned his office; the brevity of the period during which he was absent

123

counts for nothing; in the present case it is the attempt to escape that counts for everything. Never again can the nation trust a ruler who has proved derelict to his duties; has broken his oath, entered into a secret conspiracy to escape from his post, hidden the Royalty of France under the mask of a menial, made his way to a frontier full of traitors and deserters, and then intrigued for his return at the head of an army that would enable him to act as a tyrant.

Is he responsible for his departure or should we only regard as responsible those who were the companions of his flight? Was his project of escape his own voluntary act, or was it suggested by others? It really does not matter in the least what answer is given to these questions. The facts show that, if he is not a hypocrite or traitor, he must be a madman or an imbecile, and, in any case, entirely unfitted to discharge the function confided to him by the people.

Therefore, mutual obligations which may have existed between him and us are dissolved, no matter from what standpoint we view the subject. He is no longer invested with authority. He has no claim on our allegiance. There is no distinction between him and other individuals; to us he is simply Louis Capet.

The history of France is chiefly concerned with the misfortunes of the nation, and we find that the vices of kings have been the root and origin of these misfortunes; we have always been the miserable victims of monarchical oppression, sometimes being ruined by our own devotion to royalty, sometimes crushed to the earth by its tyranny. Now that treason is added to the long series of cruelties and crimes which France has had to endure at the hands of kings, the long catalogue of their awful offenses is finished; there are no more crimes left for them to commit, therefore their claim to rule is a thing of the past.

An office that may be filled by a person without talent or experience, an office that does not require virtue or wisdom, for its due exercise, an office which is the reward of birth, and which may consequently devolve on a madman, an imbecile or a tyrant, is, in the very nature of things, an absurdity, and, whatever its ostentation, has no real utility. France, which has now attained the age of reason, should no longer be deceived by mere words, and should also reflect on another aspect of the case; namely, on the peril to which the government of a king subjects a people, even when he happens to be in himself a very paltry and despicable individual.

It takes thirty millions of francs to keep the coarse state and grandeur with which the King surrounds himself. Supposing this amount were applied to the diminution of taxation, what a relief it would be to the overburdened nation, while at the same time an important source of political corruption would be eradicated. The greatness of a people is not, as monarchs claim, based on the magnificence of a king, but in the people's sense of its own dignity and on its contempt for the brutal follies and crimes which have, under the leadership of kings, desolated the whole of Europe.

There need be no alarm as to the safety of Louis Capet's person. France will not step down from her lofty position in order to retaliate her wrongs on a miserable creature who is conscious of his own dishonor. The tranquillity which exists everywhere is evidence of the fact that self-respect is the attribute of a free nation, and that, when the cause which it upholds is just and glorious, it will never allow that cause to be degraded.

TO THE ABBÉ SIEYÈS

PAINE published this open letter, dated Paris, July 8, 1791, to the Abbé (Emmanuel Joseph) Sieyès in the Paris "Moniteur," in reply to a letter of the Abbé provoked by Paine's anti-royalist declaration in "Le Républicain." The Abbé declined to enter into a controversy with Paine, and the latter presented their opposing views in the third chapter of Part Two of the "Rights of Man," in which the French statesman is quoted as arguing that "In the history of all elective monarchies . . . there is not one in which the elective mode is not worse than the hereditary succession."

The Abbé Sieyès originated the idea of the French geographical division into departments, arrondissements and communes, being himself, in 1791, member for the department of the Seine. He is credited with "discovering" Napoleon Bonaparte as a military coadjutor to cope with the Jacobin faction. Instead of being his coadjutor, Bonaparte proved to be his master.

AT the moment of my departure from England, I read in the *Moniteur* of Tuesday last, your letter, in which you give the challenge, on the subject of government, and offer to defend what is called the *monarchical opinion* against the republican system.

I accept of your challenge with pleasure; and I place such confidence in the superiority of the republican system over that nullity of a system, called *monarchy*, that I engage not to exceed the extent of fifty pages, and to leave you the liberty of taking as much latitude as you may think proper.

The respect which I bear your moral and literary reputation, will be your security for my candor in the course of this discussion; but, notwithstanding that I shall treat the subject seriously and sincerely, let me promise, that I consider myself at liberty to ridicule, as they deserve, monarchical absurdities, whensoever the occasion shall present itself.

By republicanism, I do not understand what the name signifies in Holland, and in some parts of Italy. I understand simply a government by representation —a government founded upon the principles of the Declaration of Rights; principles to which several parts of the French Constitution arise in contradiction. The Declaration of Rights of France and America are but one and the same thing in principles, and almost in expressions; and this is the republicanism which I undertake to defend against what is called *monarchy* and *aristocracy*.

I see with pleasure, that in respect to one point we are already agreed; and *that is, the extreme danger of a civil list of thirty millions.* I can discover no reason why one of the parts of the government should be supported with so extravagant a profusion, while the other scarcely receives what is sufficient for its common wants.

This dangerous and dishonorable disproportion at once supplies the one with the means of corrupting, and throws the other into the predicament of being corrupted. In America there is but little difference, with regard to this point, between the legislative and the executive part of our government; but the first is much better attended to than it is in France.

In whatsoever manner, Sir, I may treat the subject of which you have proposed the investigation, I hope that you will not doubt my entertaining for you the highest esteem. I must also add, that I am not the personal enemy of kings. Quite the contrary.

No man more heartily wishes than myself to see them all in the happy and honorable state of private individuals; but I am the avowed, open, and intrepid enemy of what is called monarchy; and I am such by principles which nothing can either alter or corrupt —by my attachment to humanity; by the anxiety which I feel within myself, for the dignity and the honor of the human race; by the disgust which I experience, when I observe men directed by children, and governed by brutes; by the horror which all the evils that monarchy has spread over the earth excite within my breast; and by those sentiments which make me shudder at the calamities, the exactions, the wars, and the massacres with which monarchy has crushed mankind: in short, it is against all the hell of monarchy that I have declared war.

THOMAS PAINE.

TO THE ATTORNEY-GENERAL

PAINE addressed this communication to the English Attorney-General, Sir Archibald Macdonald, some time in May, 1792, while he was dwelling with his publisher, Thomas Rickman, at 7 Upper Marylebone Street, London. A detailed account of the legal proceedings with regard to the publishers may be found in "Letter to the Addressers," which appears elsewhere in this volume.

The case brought by the English Government against the author of the "Rights of Man" was set down in the calendar for June 8, 1792, and on that day Paine was in court. Greatly to his disappointment, the trial was postponed to December 18, at which time he had gone to Paris to take his place in the French National Convention, to which he had been elected a delegate. His attorney of record was the Honorable Thomas Erskine.

THOUGH I have some reason for believing that you were not the original promoter or encourager of the prosecution commenced against the work entitled "Rights of Man," either as that prosecution is intended to affect the author, the publisher, or the public; yet as you appear the official person therein, I address this letter to you, not as Sir Archibald Macdonald, but as Attorney-General.

You began by a prosecution against the publisher Jordan, and the reason assigned by Mr. Secretary Dundas, in the House of Commons, in the debate on the Proclamation, May twenty-fifth, for taking that measure, was, he said, because Mr. Paine could not be found, or words to that effect. Mr. Paine, Sir, so far from secreting himself, never went a step out of

131

his way, nor in the least instance varied from his usual conduct, to avoid any measure you might choose to adopt with respect to him. It is on the purity of his heart, and the universal utility of the principles and plans which his writings contain, that he rests the issue; and he will not dishonor it by any kind of subterfuge. The apartments which he occupied at the time of writing the work, last winter, he has continued to occupy to the present hour, and the solicitors of the prosecution knew where to find him; of which there is a proof in their own office, as far back as the twenty-first of May, and also in the office of my own attorney.

But admitting, for the sake of the case, that the reason for proceeding against the publisher was, as Mr. Dundas stated, that Mr. Paine could not be found, that reason can now exist no longer.

The instant that I was informed that an information was preparing to be filed against me, as the author of, I believe, one of the most useful and benevolent books ever offered to mankind, I directed my attorney to put in an appearance; and as I shall meet the prosecution fully and fairly, and with a good and upright conscience, I have a right to expect that no act of littleness will be made use of on the part of the prosecution toward influencing the future issue with respect to the author. This expression may, perhaps, appear obscure to you, but I am in the possession of some matters which serve to show that the action against the publisher is not intended to be a *real* action. If, therefore, any persons concerned in the prosecution have found their cause so weak, as to make it appear convenient to them to enter into a negotiation with the publisher, whether for the purpose of his submitting to a verdict, and to make use of the verdict so obtained as a circumstance, by way of precedent, on a future trial against myself; or for any other purpose not fully made known to me; if, I say, I have cause to suspect this to be the case, I shall most certainly withdraw the defense I should otherwise have made, or promoted on his (the publisher's) behalf, and leave the negotiators to themselves, and shall reserve the whole of the defense for the *real* trial.

But, Sir, for the purpose of conducting this matter with at least the appearance of fairness and openness, that shall justify itself before the public, whose cause it really is (for it is the right of public discussion and investigation that is questioned), I have to propose to you to cease the prosecution against the publisher; and as the reason or pretext can no longer exist for continuing it against him because Mr. Paine could not be found, that you would direct the whole process against me, with whom the prosecuting party will not find it possible to enter into any private negotiation.

I will do the cause full justice, as well for the sake of the nation, as for my own reputation.

Another reason for discontinuing the process against the publisher is, because it can amount to nothing. First, because a jury in London cannot decide upon the fact of publishing beyond the limits of the jurisdiction of London, and therefore the work may be republished over and over again in every county in the nation, and every case must have a separate process; and by the time that three or four hundred prosecutions have been had, the eyes of the nation will then be fully open to see that the work in question contains a plan the best calculated to root out all the abuses of government, and to lessen the taxes of the nation upward of *six millions annually*.

Secondly, because though the gentlemen of London may be very expert in understanding their particular professions and occupations, and how to make business contracts with government beneficial to themselves as individuals, the rest of the nation may not be disposed to consider them sufficiently qualified nor authorized to determine for the whole nation on plans of reform, and on systems and principles of government. This would be in effect to erect a jury into a national convention, instead of electing a convention, and to lay a precedent for the probable tyranny of juries, under the pretense of supporting their rights.

That the possibility always exists of packing juries will not be denied; and, therefore, in all cases, where government is the prosecutor, more especially in those where the right of public discussion and investigation of principles and systems of government is attempted to be suppressed by a verdict, or in those where the object of the work that is prosecuted is the reform of abuse and the abolition of sinecure places and pensions, in all these cases the verdict of a jury will itself become a subject of discussion; and therefore, it furnishes an additional reason for discontinuing the prosecution against the publisher, more especially as it is not a secret that there has been a negotiation with him for secret purposes, and for proceeding against me only. I shall make a much stronger defense than what I believe the Treasury Solicitor's agreement with him will permit him to do.

I believe that Mr. Burke, finding himself defeated, and not being able to make any answer to the "Rights of Man," has been one of the promoters of this prosecution; and I shall return the compliment to him by showing, in a future publication, that he has been a masked pensioner at £1500 per annum for about ten years.

Thus it is that the public money is wasted, and the dread of public investigation is produced.

I am, sir,

Your obedient humble servant,

THOMAS PAINE.

TO MR. SECRETARY DUNDAS

THE recipient of this tart communication, dated London, June 6, 1792, was a British statesman of Scotch lineage, Henry D. Dundas, afterwards Viscount Melville, who, in 1791, had been appointed Home Secretary and who had previously been active in procuring the impeachment of Warren Hastings. Dundas was officially intolerant of any criticism levelled against existing government in Britain, and was rewarded by being made Secretary of War and, in 1804, First Lord of the Admiralty under Pitt. The ensuing year he was impeached, by the House of Lords, "of high crimes and misdemeanors" in his management of naval finances; but eventually was acquitted. A short time after the prosecution of the "Rights of Man," Secretary Dundas, ever a reactionary, gained notoriety by his rigorous prosecutions of the Scotch radicals in 1795. In this document Paine disregarded friendly advice in referring to George the Third as "King or Madjesty," in punning allusion to his mental infirmity.

AS you opened the debate in the House of Commons, May twenty-fifth, on the proclamation for suppressing publications, which that proclamation (without naming any) calls wicked and seditious: and as you applied those opprobrious epithets to the works entitled "Rights of Man," I think it unnecessary to offer any other reason for addressing this letter to you.

I begin, then, at once, by declaring, that I do not believe there are found in the writings of any author, ancient or modern, on the subject of government, a spirit of greater benignity, and a stronger inculcation of moral principles than in those which I have published. They come, Sir, from a man, who, by having lived in different countries, and under different systems of government, and who, being intimate in the construction of them, is a better judge of the subject than it is possible that you, from the want of those opportunities, can be: and besides this, they come from a heart that knows not how to beguile.

I will further say, that when that moment arrives in which the best consolation that shall be left will be looking back on some past actions, more virtuous and more meritorious than the rest, I shall then with happiness remember, among other things, I have written the "Rights of Man." As to what proclamations, or prosecutions, or place-men, and place-expectants—those who possess, or those who are gaping for office—may say of them, it will not alter their character, either with the world or with me.

Having, Sir, made this declaration, I shall proceed to remark, not particularly on your speech on that occasion, but on any one to which your motion on that day gave rise; and I shall begin with that of Mr. Adam.

This gentleman accuses me of not having done the very thing that *I have done,* and which, he says, if I *had* done, he should not have accused me.

Mr. Adam, in his speech (see the *Morning Chronicle* of May 26), says,

> That he had well considered the subject of constitutional publications, and was by no means ready to say (but the contrary) that books of science upon government though recommending a doctrine or system different from the form of our Constitution (meaning that of England) were fit objects of prosecution; that if he did, he must condemn HARRINGTON for his "Oceana," SIR THOMAS MORE for his "Utopia," and HUME for his "Idea of a Perfect Commonwealth." But (continued Mr. Adam) the publication of Mr. PAINE was very different; for it reviled what was most sacred in the Constitution, destroyed every principle of subordination, and *established nothing in their room.*

I readily perceive that Mr. Adam has not read the second part of "Rights of Man," and I am put under the necessity, either of submitting to an erroneous charge, or of justifying myself against it; and certainly shall prefer the latter. If, then, I shall prove to Mr. Adam, that in my reasoning upon systems of government, in the second part of "Rights of Man," I have shown as clearly, I think, as words can convey ideas, a certain system of government, and that not existing in theory only, but already in full and established practise, and systematically and practically free from all the vices and defects of the English Government, and capable of producing more happiness to the people, and that also with an eightieth part of the taxes, which the present English system of government consumes; I hope he will do me the justice, when he next goes to the House, to get up and confess he had been mistaken in saying, that I had *established nothing, and that I had destroyed every principle of subordination.* Having thus opened the case, I now come to the point.

In the second part of the "Rights of Man," I have distinguished government into two classes or systems: the one the hereditary system, the other the representative system.

In the first part of "Rights of Man," I have endeavored to show, and I challenge any man to refute it, that there does not exist a right to establish hereditary government; or, in other words, hereditary governors; because hereditary government always means a government yet to come, and the case always is, that the people who are to live afterwards, have always the same right to choose a government for themselves, as the people had who lived before them.

In the second part of "Rights of Man," I have not repeated those arguments, because they are irrefutable; but have confined myself to show the defects of what is called hereditary government, or hereditary succession, that it must, from the nature of it, throw government into the hands of men totally unworthy of it, from want of principle, or unfitted for it from want of capacity. James II is recorded as an instance of the first of these cases; and instances are to be found almost all over Europe to prove the truth of the latter.

To show the absurdity of the hereditary system still more strongly, I will now put the following case: Take any fifty men promiscuously, and it will be very extraordinary if, out of that number, one man should be found, whose principles and talents taken together (for some might have principles, and others might have talents) would render him a person truly fitted to fill any very extraordinary office of national trust. If then such a fitness of character could not be expected to be found in more than one person out of fifty, it would happen but once in a thousand years to the eldest son of any one family, admitting each, on an average, to hold the office twenty years. Mr. Adam talks of something in the Constitution which he calls *most sacred*; but I hope he does not mean hereditary succession, a thing which appears to me a violation of every order of nature, and of common sense.

When I look into history and see the multitudes of men, otherwise virtuous, who have died, and their families been ruined, in the defense of knaves and fools, and which they would not have done, had they reasoned at all upon the system; I do not know a greater good that an individual can render to mankind, than to endeavor to break the chains of political superstition. Those chains are now dissolving fast, and proclamations and persecutions will serve but to hasten that dissolution.

Having thus spoken of the hereditary system as a bad system, and subject to every possible defect, I now come to the representative system, and this Mr. Adam will find stated in the second part of "Rights of Man," not only as the best, but as the only *theory* of government under which the liberties of the people can be permanently secure.

But it is needless now to talk of mere theory, since there is already a government in full practise, established upon that theory; or in other words, upon the "Rights of Man," and has been so for almost twenty years. Mr. Pitt, in a speech of his some short time since, said, "That there never did, and never could exist a government established upon those rights, and that if it began at noon, it would end at night." Mr. Pitt has not yet arrived at the degree of a schoolboy in this species of knowledge; his practise has been confined to the means of *extorting revenue,* and his boast has been—*how much!* Whereas the boast of the system of government that I am speaking of, is not how much, but how little.

The system of government purely representative, unmixed with anything of hereditary nonsense, began in America. I will now compare the effects of that system of government with the system of government in England, both during, and since the close of the war.

So powerful is the representative system, first, by combining and consolidating all the parts of a country together, however great the extent; and, secondly, by admitting of none but men properly qualified into the government, or dismissing them if they prove to be otherwise, that America was enabled thereby totally to defeat and overthrow all the schemes and projects of the hereditary Government of England against her. As the establishment of the Revolution and Independence of America is a proof of this fact, it is needless to enlarge upon it.

I now come to the comparative effect of the two systems *since* the close of the war, and I request Mr. Adam to attend to it.

America had internally sustained the ravages of upwards of seven years of war, which England had not. England sustained only the expense of the war; whereas America sustained not only the expense, but the destruction of property committed by *both* armies. Not a house was built during that period, and many thousands were destroyed. The farms and plantations along the coast of the country, for more than a thousand miles, were laid waste. Her commerce was annihilated. Her ships were either taken, or had rotted within her own harbors. The credit of her funds had fallen upwards of ninety per cent, that is, an original hundred pounds would not sell for ten pounds. In fine, she was apparently put back a hundred years when the war closed, which was not the case with England.

But such was the event, that the same representative system of government, though since better organized, which enabled her to conquer, enabled her also to recover, and she now presents a more flourishing condition, and a more happy and harmonized society, under that system of government, than any country in the world can boast under any other. Her towns are rebuilt, much better than before; her farms and plantations are in higher improvement than ever; her commerce is spread over the world, and her funds have risen from less than ten pounds the hundred to upwards of one hundred and twenty. Mr. Pitt and his colleagues talk of the things that have happened in his boyish administration, without knowing what greater things have happened elsewhere, and under other systems of government.

I now come to state the expense of the two systems, as they now stand in each of the countries; but it may first be proper to observe, that government in America is what it ought to be, a matter of honor and trust, and not made a trade of for the purpose of lucre.

The whole amount of the net taxes in England (exclusive of the expense of collection, of drawbacks, of seizures and condemnation, of fines and penalties, of fees of office, of litigations and informers, which are some of the blessed means of enforcing them) is seventeen millions. Of thus sum, about nine millions go for the payment of the interest of the national debt, and the remainder, being about eight millions, is for the current annual expenses. This much for one side of the case. I now come to the other.

The expense of the several departments of the general Representative Government of the United States of America, extending over a space of country nearly ten times larger than England, is $294,558, which, at 4s. 6d. per dollar, is £66,305, 11s. sterling, and is thus apportioned:

Expense of the Executive Department.

	£	s.
The Office of Presidency, for which the President receives nothing for himself	5,625	0
Vice President	1,125	0
Chief-justice	900	0
Five associate Justices	3,937	10
Nineteen Judges of Districts, and Attorney-General..	6,873	15

Legislative Department.

Members of Congress at 6 dolls. (1*l.* 7*s.*) per day, their Secretaries, Clerks, Chaplains, Messengers, Door-keepers, etc.	25,515	0

Treasury Department.

Secretary, Assistant, Comptroller, Auditor, Treasurer, Register, and Loan-Office Keeper, in each state, together with all necessary Clerks, Office Keepers, etc.	12,825	0

Department of State, including Foreign Affairs.

Secretary, Clerks, etc., etc.	1,406	5

Department of War.

Secretary, Clerks, Paymasters, Commissioners, etc..	1,462	10

Commissioners for settling Old Accounts.

The whole Board, Clerks, etc.	2,598	15

Incidental and Contingent expenses.

For Fire-wood, Stationery, Printing, etc.	4,006	16

Total.......... 66,275 11

On account of the incursions of the Indians on the back settlements, Congress is at this time obliged to keep six thousand militia in pay, in addition to a regiment of foot, and a battalion of artillery, which it always keeps; and this increases the expense of the War Department to $390,000 which is £87,795 sterling, but when peace shall be concluded with the Indians, the greatest part of this expense will cease, and the total amount of the expense of government, including that of the army, will not amount to £100,-000 sterling, which, as has been already stated, is but an eightieth part of the expenses of the English Government.

I request Mr. Adam and Mr. Dundas, and all those who are talking of constitutions, and blessings, and kings, and lords, and the Lord knows what, to look at this statement. Here is a form and system of government that is better organized and better administered than any government in the world, and that for less than one £100,000 per annum, and yet every Member of Congress receives, as a compensation for his time and attendance on public business, one pound seven shillings per day, which is at the rate of nearly £500 a year.

This is a government that has nothing to fear. It needs no proclamations to deter people from writing and reading. It needs no political superstition to support it; it was by encouraging discussion and rendering the press free upon all subjects of government, that the principles of government became understood in America, and the people are now enjoying the present blessings under it. You hear of no riots, tumults, and disorders in that country; because there exists no cause to produce them. Those things are never the effect of freedom, but of restraint, oppression, and excessive taxation.

In America there is not that class of poor and wretched people that are so numerously dispersed all over England, who are to be told by a proclamation, that they are happy; and this is in a great measure to be accounted for, not by the difference of proclamations, but by the difference of governments and the difference of taxes between that country and this. What the laboring people of that country earn, they apply to their own use, and to the education of their children, and do not pay it away in taxes as fast as they earn it, to support court extravagance, and a long enormous list of place-men and pensioners; and besides this, they have learned the manly doctrine of reverencing themselves, and consequently of respecting each other; and they laugh at those imaginary beings called kings and lords, and all the fraudulent trumpery of court.

When place-men and pensioners, or those who expect to be such, are lavish in praise of a government, it is not a sign of its being a good one. The pension list alone in England (see Sir John Sinclair's "History of the Revenue," p. 6, of the Appendix) is £107,-404, *which is more than the expenses of the whole Government of America amount to.* And I am now more convinced than before, that the offer that was made to me of a thousand pounds for the copyright of the second part of the "Rights of Man," together with the remaining copyright of the first part, was to have effected, by a quick suppression, what is now attempted to be done by a prosecution. The connection which the person, who made the offer, has with the King's printing office, may furnish part of the means of inquiring into this affair, when the Ministry shall please to bring their prosecution to issue. But to return to my subject.

I have said in the second part of the "Rights of Man," and I repeat it here, that the service of any man, whether called king, president, senator, legislator, or anything else cannot be worth more to any country in the regular routine of office, than £10,000 per annum. We have a better man in America, and more of a gentleman, than any king I ever knew of, who does not occasion half that expense; for, though the salary is fixed at £5,625 he does not accept it, and it is only the incidental expenses that are paid out of it. The name by which a man is called is of itself but an empty thing. It is worth and character alone which can render him valuable, for without these, kings, and lords, and presidents, are but jingling names.

But without troubling myself about constitutions of government, I have shown in the second part of "Rights of Man," that an alliance may be formed between England, France, and America and that the expenses of government in England may be put back to one million and a half, viz.:

Civil expense of government	£500,000
Army	500,000
Navy	500,000
Total	£1,500,000

And even this sum is fifteen times greater than the expenses of government are in America; and it is also greater than the whole peace establishment of England amounted to about a hundred years ago. So much has the weight and oppression of taxes increased since the Revolution, and especially since the year 1714.

To show that the sum of £500,000 is sufficient to defray all civil expenses of government, I have, in that work, annexed the following estimate for any country of the same extent as England.

In the first place, three hundred representatives, fairly elected, are sufficient for all the purposes to which legislation can apply, and preferable to a larger number.

If, then, an allowance, at the rate of £500 per annum be made to every representative, deducting for non-attendance, the expense, if the whole number attended six months each year, would be £75,000.

The official departments could not possibly exceed the following number, with the salaries annexed, viz.:

Three offices	at	£10,000	each	£30,000
Ten ditto	at	5,000	"	50,000
Twenty ditto	at	2,000	"	40,000
Forty ditto	at	1,000	"	40,000
Two hundred ditto	at	500	"	100,000
Three hundred ditto	at	200	"	60,000
Five hundred ditto	at	100	"	50,000
Seven hundred ditto	at	75	"	52,500
				£422,500

If a nation chose, it might deduct four per cent from all the offices, and make one of £20,000 per annum, and style the person who should fill it, king or majesty, or give him any other title.

Taking, however, this sum of one million and a half, as an abundant supply for all the expenses of government under any form whatever, there will remain a surplus of nearly six millions and a half out of the present taxes, after paying the interest of the national debt; and I have shown in the second part of the "Rights of Man," what appears to me, the best mode of applying the surplus money; for I am now speaking of expenses and savings, and not of systems of government.

I have, in the first place, estimated the poor-rates at two millions annually, and shown that the first effectual step would be to abolish the poor-rates entirely (which would be a saving of two millions to the housekeepers), and to remit four millions out of the surplus taxes to the poor, to be paid to them in money, in proportion to the number of children in each family, and the number of aged persons.

I have estimated the number of persons of both sexes in England, of fifty years of age and upwards, at 420,000, and have taken one-third of this number, viz, 140,000, to be poor people.

To save long calculations, I have taken 70,000 of them to be upwards of fifty years of age, and under sixty, and the others to be sixty years and upwards; and to allow six pounds per annum to the former class, and ten pounds per annum to the latter. The expense of which will be:

70,000 persons at £6 per annum................	£420,000
70,000 persons at £10 per annum................	700,000
	£1,120,000

There will then remain of the four millions, £2,880,000. I have stated two different methods of appropriating this money. The one is to pay it in proportion to the number of children in each family, at the rate of three or four pounds per annum for each child; the other is to apportion it according to the expense of living in different counties; but in either of these cases it would, together with the allowance to be made to the aged, completely take off taxes from one-third of all the families in England, besides relieving all the other families from the burden of poor-rates.

The whole number of families in England, allotting five souls to each family, is 1,400,000, of which I take one third, viz, 466,666, to be poor families who now pay four millions of taxes, and that the poorest pays at least four guineas a year; and that the other thirteen millions are paid by the other two-thirds.

The plan, therefore, as stated in the work, is, first, to remit or repay, as is already stated, this sum of four millions to the poor, because it is impossible to separate them from the others in the present mode of collecting taxes on articles of consumption; and, secondly, to abolish the poor-rates, the house and window-light tax, and to change the commutation tax into a progressive tax on large estates, the particulars of all which are set forth in the work, to which I desire Mr. Adam to refer for particulars. I shall here content myself with saying, that to a town of the population of Manchester, it will make a difference in its favor, compared with the present state of things, of upwards of £50,000 annually, and so in proportion to all other places throughout the nation. This certainly is of more consequence than that the same sums should be collected to be afterwards spent by riotous and profligate courtiers, and in nightly revels at the Star and Garter tavern, Pall Mall.

I will conclude this part of my letter with an extract from the second part of the "Rights of Man," which Mr. Dundas (a man rolling in luxury at the expense of the nation) has branded with the epithet of "wicked."

By the operation of this plan, the poor laws, those instruments of civil torture, will be superseded, and the wasteful ex-

pense of litigation prevented. The hearts of the humane will
not be shocked by ragged and hungry children, and persons of
seventy and eighty years of age begging for bread. The dying
poor will not be dragged from place to place to breathe their
last, as a reprisal of parish upon parish. Widows will have
a maintenance for their children, and not be carted away, on
the death of their husbands, like culprits and criminals; and
children will no longer be considered as increasing the distresses
of their parents. The haunts of the wretched will be known,
because it will be to their advantage; and the number of petty
crimes, the offspring of poverty and distress, will be lessened.
The poor as well as the rich will then be interested in the support of government, and the cause and apprehension of riots
and tumults will cease. Ye who sit in ease, and solace yourselves in plenty, and such there are in Turkey and Russia, as
well as in England, and who say to yourselves, *are we not well
off?* have ye thought of these things? When ye do, ye will cease
to speak and feel for yourselves alone.

After this remission of four millions be made, and
the poor-rates and houses and window-light tax be
abolished, and the commutation tax changed, there
will still remain nearly one million and a half of surplus taxes; and as by an alliance between England,
France and America, armies and navies will, in a
great measure, be rendered unnecessary; and as men
who have either been brought up in, or long habited
to those lines of life, are still citizens of a nation in
common with the rest, and have a right to participate
in all plans of national benefit, it is stated in that work
("Rights of Man," Part II) to apply annually £507,-

000 out of the surplus taxes to this purpose, in the following manner:

To 15,000 disbanded soldiers, 3s. per week (clear of deduction) during life	£117,000
Additional pay to the remaining soldiers, per annum	19,500
To the officers of the disbanded corps, during life, the sum of	117,000
To 15,000 disbanded sailors, 3s. per week during life	117,000
Additional pay to the remaining sailors	19,500
To the officers of the disbanded part of the navy, during life	117,000
	£507,000

The limits to which it is proper to confine this letter, will not admit of my entering into further particulars. I address it to Mr. Dundas because he took the lead in the debate, and he wishes, I suppose, to appear conspicuous; but the purport of it is to justify myself from the charge which Mr. Adam has made.

This gentleman, as has been observed in the beginning of this letter, considers the writings of Harrington, More and Hume, as justifiable and legal publications, because they reasoned by comparison, though in so doing they showed plans and systems of government, not only different from, but preferable to, that of England; and he accuses me of endeavoring to confuse, instead of producing a system in the room of that which I had reasoned against;

whereas, the fact is, that I have not only reasoned by comparison of the representative system against the hereditary system, but I have gone further; for I have produced an instance of a government established entirely on the representative system, under which greater happiness is enjoyed, much fewer taxes required, and much higher credit is established, than under the system of government in England. The funds in England have risen since the war only from £54 to £97 and they have been down since the Proclamation to £87, whereas the funds in America rose in the meantime from £10 to £120.

His charge against me of "destroying every principle of subordination," is equally as groundless; which even a single paragraph from the work will prove, and which I shall here quote:

> Formerly when divisions arose respecting governments, recourse was had to the sword, and a civil war ensued. That savage custom is exploded by the new system, and *recourse is had to a national convention*. Discussion, and the general will, arbitrates the question, and to this private opinion yields with a good grace, and *order is preserved uninterrupted*.

That two different charges should be brought at the same time, the one by a member of the Legislature, for *not* doing a certain thing, and the other by the Attorney-general for *doing* it, is a strange jumble

of contradictions. I have now justified myself, or
the work rather, against the first, by stating the case
in this letter, and the justification of the other will
be undertaken in its proper place. But in any case
the work will go on.

I shall now conclude this letter with saying, that
the only objection I found against the plan and principles contained in the second part of "Rights of
Man," when I had written the book, was, that they
would beneficially interest at least ninety-nine persons out of every hundred throughout the nation, and
therefore would not leave sufficient room for men to
act from the direct and disinterested principles of
honor; but the prosecution now commenced has fortunately removed that objection, and the approvers and
protectors of that work now feel the immediate impulse of honor added to that of national interest.

I am, Mr. Dundas,

Not your obedient humble servant,

But the contrary,

THOMAS PAINE.

LETTERS TO ONSLOW CRANLEY

Lord Lieutenant of the County of Surrey; on the subject of the late excellent PROCLAMATION:—*or the* CHAIRMAN *who shall preside at the meeting to be held at Epsom, June eighteenth.*

FIRST LETTER, DATED AT LONDON, JUNE 17, 1792.

PERSISTENTLY Thomas Paine sought with every weapon of speech at his command to assure his critics that the "Rights of Man" was a protest against hereditary, as contrasted with elective, government. This, of course, being a direct blow at English royalty, was antagonistic to all the ministers and sycophants of the crown, including the Lord Onslow to whom these letters were addressed.

Paine was constantly fighting with his pen in behalf of the "tax-paying under-dog." In these letters to Onslow Cranley he makes no excuse for his attitude and principles, but, on the contrary, has the "honor and happiness to be the author" of the "Rights of Man."

Irony and sarcasm have seldom been wielded with such telling literary force as in the second of these letters, in which Paine condemns men like Cranley for "living in indolence and luxury, on the labors of the public."

SIR: I have seen in the public newspapers the following advertisement, to-wit:

To the Nobility, Gentry, Clergy, Freeholders, and other inhabitants of the County of Surrey.

At the requisition and desire of several of the freeholders of the county, I am, in the absence of the sheriff, to desire the favor of your attendance, at a meeting to be held at Epsom, on Monday, the eighteenth instant, at twelve o'clock at noon, to consider of an humble address to His Majesty, to express our grateful approbation of His Majesty's paternal, and well-timed attendance to the public welfare, in his late most gracious Proclamation against the enemies of our happy Constitution.

(Signed.) ONSLOW CRANLEY.

Taking it for granted, that the aforesaid advertisement, equally as obscure as the Proclamation to

159

which it refers, has nevertheless some meaning, and is intended to effect some purpose; and as a prosecution (whether wisely or unwisely, justly or unjustly) is already commenced against a work entitled "Rights of Man," of which I have the honor and happiness to be the author; I feel it necessary to address this letter to you, and to request that it may be read publicly to the gentlemen who shall meet at Epsom in consequence of the advertisement.

The work now under prosecution is, I conceive, the same work which is intended to be suppressed by the aforesaid Proclamation. Admitting this to be the case, the gentlemen of the County of Surrey are called upon by somebody to condemn a work, and they are at the same time forbidden by the Proclamation to know what that work is; and they are further called upon to give their aid and assistance to prevent other people from knowing it also. It is therefore necessary that the author, for his own justification, as well as to prevent the gentlemen who shall meet from being imposed upon by misrepresentation, should give some outlines of the principles and plans which that work contains.

The work, Sir, in question, contains, first, an investigation of general principles of government.

It also distinguishes government into two classes
or systems, the one the hereditary system; the other
the representative system; and it compares these two
systems with each other.

It shows that what is called hereditary government
cannot exist as a matter of right; because hereditary
government always means a government yet to come;
and the case always is, that those who are to live afterwards have always the same right to establish a government for themselves as the people who had lived
before them.

It also shows the defect to which hereditary government is unavoidably subject: that it must, from
the nature of it, throw government into the hands of
men totally unworthy of it from the want of principle, and unfitted for it from want of capacity.
James II and many others are recorded in the English
history as proofs of the former of those cases, and
instances are to be found all over Europe to prove
the truth of the latter.

It then shows that the representative system is the
only true system of government; that it is also the
only system under which the liberties of any people
can be permanently secure; and, further, that it is the
only one that can continue the same equal probability at all times of admitting of none but men

properly qualified, both by principles and abilities, into government, and of excluding such as are otherwise.

The work shows also, by plans and calculations not hitherto denied nor controverted, not even by the prosecution that is commenced, that the taxes now existing may be reduced at least six millions, that taxes may be entirely taken off from the poor, who are computed at one third of the nation; and that taxes on the other two-thirds may be considerably reduced; that the aged poor may be comfortably provided for, and the children of poor families properly educated; that fifteen thousand soldiers, and the same number of sailors, may be allowed three shillings per week during life out of the surplus taxes; and also that a proportionate allowance may be made to the officers, and the pay of the remaining soldiers and sailors be raised; and that it is better to apply the surplus taxes to those purposes, than to consume them on lazy and profligate placemen and pensioners; and that the revenue, said to be twenty thousand pounds per annum, raised by a tax upon coals, and given to the Duke of Richmond, is a gross imposition upon all the people of London, and ought to be instantly abolished.

This, Sir, is a concise abstract of the principles and plans contained in the work that is now prosecuted, and for the suppression of which the Proclamation appears to be intended; but as it is impossible that I can, in the compass of a letter, bring into view all the matters contained in the work, and as it is proper that the gentlemen who may compose that meeting should know what the merits or demerits of it are, before they come to any resolutions, either directly or indirectly relating thereto, I request the honor of presenting them with one hundred copies of the second part of the "Rights of Man," and also one thousand copies of my letter to Mr. Dundas, which I have directed to be sent to Epsom for that purpose; and I beg the favor of the chairman to take the trouble of presenting them to the gentlemen who shall meet on that occasion, with my sincere wishes for their happiness, and for that of the nation in general.

Having now closed thus much of the subject of my letter, I next come to speak of what has relation to me personally. I am well aware of the delicacy that attends it, but the purpose of calling the meeting appears to me so inconsistent with that justice that is always due between man and man, that it is proper

I should (as well on account of the gentlemen who may meet, as on my own account) explain myself fully and candidly thereon.

I have already informed the gentlemen, that a prosecution is commenced against a work of which I have the honor and happiness to be the author; and I have good reasons for believing that the Proclamation which the gentlemen are called to consider, and to present an address upon, is purposely calculated to give an impression to the jury before whom that matter is to come. In short, that it is dictating a verdict by proclamation; and I consider the instigators of the meeting to be held at Epsom, as aiding and abetting the same improper, and, in my opinion, illegal purpose, and that in a manner very artfully contrived, as I shall now show.

Had a meeting been called of the Freeholders of the County of Middlesex, the gentlemen who had composed that meeting would have rendered themselves objectionable as persons to serve on a jury, before whom a judicial case was afterwards to come. But by calling a meeting out of the County of Middlesex, that matter is artfully avoided, and the gentlemen of Surrey are summoned, as if it were intended thereby to give a tone to the sort of verdict which the instigators of the meeting no doubt wish should be brought in, and to give countenance to the jury in so doing.

I am, sir,
With much respect to the
Gentlemen who shall meet,
Their and your obedient and humble servant,
THOMAS PAINE.

TO ONSLOW CRANLEY

Commonly Called Lord Onslow

Second Letter, Dated at London, June 21, 1792.

SIR: When I wrote you the letter which Mr. Horne Tooke did me the favor to present to you, as chairman of the meeting held at Epsom, Monday, June 18, it was not with much expectation that you would do me the justice of permitting or recommending it to be publicly read. I am well aware that the signature of Thomas Paine has something in it dreadful to sinecure placemen and pensioners; and when you, on seeing the letter opened, informed the meeting that it was signed Thomas Paine, and added in a note of exclamation, "the common enemy of us all," you spoke one of the greatest truths you ever uttered, if you confine the expression to men of the same description with yourself; men living in indolence and luxury, on the spoil and labors of the public.

The letter has since appeared in the *Argus,* and probably in other papers. It will justify itself; but if anything on that account has been wanting, your conduct at the meeting would have supplied the omission. You there sufficiently proved that I was not mistaken in supposing that the meeting was called to give an indirect aid to the prosecution commenced against a work, the reputation of which will long outlive the memory of the Pensioner I am writing to.

When meetings, Sir, are called by the partizans of the Court, to preclude the nation the right of investigating systems and principles of government, and of exposing errors and defects, under the pretense of prosecuting an individual—it furnishes an additional motive for maintaining sacred that violated right.

The principles and arguments contained in the work in question, "Rights of Man," have stood, and they now stand, and I believe ever will stand, unrefuted. They are stated in a fair and open manner to the world, and they have already received the public approbation of a greater number of men, of the best of characters, of every denomination of religion, and of every rank in life (placemen and pensioners excepted) than all the juries that shall meet in England for ten years to come, will amount to; and I have, moreover, good reasons for believing that the approvers of that work, as well private as public, are already more numerous than all the present electors throughout the nation.

Not less than forty pamphlets, intended as answers thereto, have appeared, and as suddenly disappeared; scarcely are the titles of any of them remembered, notwithstanding their endeavors have been aided by all the daily abuse which the court and ministerial newspapers, for almost a year and a half, could bestow, both upon the work and the author; and now that every attempt to refute, and every abuse has failed, the invention of calling the work a libel has been hit upon, and the discomfited party has pusillanimously retreated to prosecution and a jury, and obscure addresses.

As I well know that a long letter from me will not be agreeable to you, I will relieve your uneasiness by making it as short as I conveniently can; and will conclude it with taking up the subject at that part where Mr. Horne Tooke was interrupted from going on when at the meeting.

That gentleman was stating, that the situation you stood in rendered it improper for you to appear *actively* in a scene in which your private interest was too visible: that you were a bedchamber lord at a thousand a year, and a pensioner at three thousand pounds a year more—and here he was stopped by the little but noisy circle you had collected round. Permit me then, Sir, to add an explanation to his words, for the benefit of your neighbors, and with which, and a few observations, I shall close my letter.

When it was reported in the English newspapers, some short time since that the Empress of Russia had given to one of her minions a large tract of country and several thousands of peasants as property, it very justly provoked indignation and abhorrence in those who heard it. But if we compare the mode practised in England, with that which appears to us so abhorrent in Russia, it will be found to amount to very near the same thing;—for example—

As the whole of the revenue in England is drawn by taxes from the pockets of the people, those things called gifts and grants (of which kind are all pensions and sinecure places) are paid out of that stock. The difference, therefore, between the two modes is, that in England the money is collected by the government, and then given to the pensioner, and in Russia he is left to collect it for himself.

The smallest sum which the poorest family in a county so near London as Surrey, can be supposed to pay annually, of taxes, is not less than five pounds and as your sinecure of one thousand, and pension of three thousand per annum, are made up of taxes paid by eight hundred such poor families, it comes to the same thing as if the eight hundred families had been given to you, as in Russia, and you had collected the money on your account. Were you to say that you are not quartered particularly on the people of Surrey, but on the nation at large, the objection would amount to nothing; for as there are more pensioners than counties, every one may be considered as quartered on that in which he lives.

What honor or happiness you can derive from being the PRINCIPAL PAUPER of the neighborhood, and occasioning a greater expense than the poor, the aged, and the infirm, for ten miles round you, I leave you to enjoy. At the same time I can see that it is no wonder you should be strenuous in suppressing a book which strikes at the root of those abuses. No wonder that you should be against reforms, against the freedom of the press, and the right of investigation. To you, and to others of your description, these are dreadful things; but you should also consider, that the motives which prompt you to *act*, ought, by reflection, to compel you to be *silent*.

Having now returned your compliment, and sufficiently tired your patience, I take my leave of you, with mentioning, that if you had not prevented my former letter from being read at the meeting, you would not have had the trouble of reading this; and also with requesting, that the next time you call me "*a common enemy,*" you would add, "*of us sinecure placemen and pensioners.*"

I am, Sir, etc., etc., etc.,

THOMAS PAINE.

TO THE

SHERIFF OF THE COUNTY OF SUSSEX

OR

The Gentleman Who Shall Preside at the Meeting to be Held at Lewes, July Fourth

Dated at London, June 30, 1792.

SO ludicrously did the attempt of the British Government to suppress the "Rights of Man" strike its author that his frequent toast was, "The best way of advertising good books—by prosecution." At the same time, Paine was something of an advertising genius himself, and never failed to secure such publicity as offered.

The accompanying letter is a case in point. Paine's object in writing it was to advertise his cause. He goes so far as naïvely to "request the sheriff, or any other person, to read this letter publicly to the company who shall assemble . . . to hear an address on the late Proclamation for suppressing writings, books, etc."

SIR: I have seen in the Lewes newspapers, of June twenty-fifth, an advertisement, signed by sundry persons, and also by the sheriff, for holding a meeting at the town-hall of Lewes, for the purpose, as the advertisement states, of presenting an address on the late Proclamation for suppressing writings, books, etc. And as I conceive that a certain publication of mine, entitled "Rights of Man," in which, among other things, the enormous increase of taxes, placemen, and pensioners, is shown to be unnecessary and oppressive, *is the*

173

particular writing alluded to in the said publication; I request the sheriff, or in his absence, whoever shall preside at the meeting, or any other person, to read this letter publicly to the company who shall assemble in consequence of that advertisement.

GENTLEMEN—It is now upwards of eighteen years since I was a resident inhabitant of the town of Lewes. My situation among you, as an officer of the revenue, for more than six years, enabled me to see into the numerous and various distresses which the weight of taxes even at that time of day occasioned; and feeling, as I then did, and as it is natural for me to do, for the hard condition of others, it is with pleasure I can declare, and every person then under my sur-vey, and now living, can witness, the exceeding can-dor, and even tenderness, with which that part of the duty that fell to my share was executed. The name of *Thomas Paine* is not to be found in the records of the Lewes' justices, in any one act of contention with, or severity of any kind whatever toward, the persons whom he surveyed, either in the town, or in the country; of this, *Mr. Fuller* and *Mr. Shelley,* who will probably attend the meeting, can, if they please, give full testimony. It is, however, not in their power to contradict it.

Having thus indulged myself in recollecting a place where I formerly had, and even now have, many friends, rich and poor, and most probably some enemies, I proceed to the more important purport of my letter.

Since my departure from Lewes, fortune or providence has thrown me into a line of action, which my first setting out into life could not possibly have suggested to me.

I have seen the fine and fertile country of America ravaged and deluged in blood, and the taxes of England enormously increased and multiplied in consequence thereof; and this, in a great measure, by the instigation of the same class of placemen, pensioners, and court dependents, who are now promoting addresses throughout England, on the present *unintelligible* Proclamation.

I have also seen a system of government rise up in that country, free from corruption, and now administered over an extent of territory ten times as large as England, *for less expense than the pensions alone in England amount to;* and under which more freedom is enjoyed, and a more happy state of society is preserved, and a more general prosperity is promoted, than under any other system of government now existing in the world. Knowing, as I do, the things I now declare, I should reproach myself with want of duty and affection to mankind, were I not in the most undismayed manner to publish them, as it were, on the house-tops, for the good of others.

Having thus glanced at what has passed within my knowledge since my leaving Lewes, I come to the subject more immediately before the meeting now present.

Mr. Edmund Burke, who, as I shall show, in a future publication, has lived a concealed pensioner, at the expense of the public of fifteen hundred pounds per annum, for about ten years last past, published a book the winter before last, in open violation of the principles of liberty, and for which he was applauded by that class of men *who are now promoting addresses*. Soon after his book appeared, I published the first part of the work, entitled "Rights of Man," as an answer thereto, and had the happiness of receiving the public thanks of several bodies of men, and of numerous individuals of the best character, of every denomination in religion, and of every rank in life—placemen and pensioners excepted.

In February last, I published the second part of "Rights of Man," and as it met with still greater approbation from the true friends of national freedom, and went deeper into the system of government, and exposed the abuses of it, more than had been done in the first part, it consequently excited an alarm among all those, who, insensible of the burden of taxes which the general mass of the people sustain, are living in luxury and indolence, and hunting after court preferments, sinecure places, and pensions, either for themselves, or for their family connections.

I have shown in that work, that the taxes may be reduced at least *six millions,* and even then the expenses of government in England would be twenty times greater than they are in the country I have already spoken of. That taxes may be entirely taken off from the poor, by remitting to them in money at the rate of between *three and four pounds* per head per annum, for the education and bringing up of the children of the poor families, who are computed at one third of the whole nation, and *six pounds* per annum to all poor persons, decayed tradesmen, or others, from the age of fifty until sixty, and *ten pounds* per annum from after sixty. And that in consequence of this allowance, to be paid out of the surplus taxes, the poor-rates would become unnecessary, and that it is better to apply the surplus taxes to these beneficent purposes, *than to waste them on idle and profligate courtiers, placemen and pensioners.*

These, gentlemen, are a part of the plans and principles contained in the work, which this meeting is now called upon, in an indirect manner, to vote an address against, and brand with the name of *wicked* and *seditious*. . . .

Gentlemen, I have now stated to you such matters as appear necessary to me to offer to the consideration of the meeting. I have no other interest in what I am doing, nor in writing you this letter, than the interest of the *heart*. I consider the proposed address as calculated to give countenance to placemen, pensioners, enormous taxation and corruption. Many of you will recollect that, while I resided among you, there was not a man more firm and open in supporting the principles of liberty than myself, and I still pursue, and ever will, the same path.

I have, gentlemen, only one request to make, which is—that those who have called the meeting will speak *out*, and say, whether in the address they are going to present against publications, which the proclamation calls wicked, they mean the work entitled "Rights of Man," or whether they do not?

I am, Gentlemen,

With sincere wishes for your happiness,

Your friend and servant,

THOMAS PAINE.

TO MR. SECRETARY DUNDAS

T HIS second letter to Dundas (dated from Calais, France, September 15, 1792), does not intimate what a narrow escape Paine had from "capture and the scaffold" in England for having written the "Rights of Man." It curiously, if not ironically, recounts to the English Home Secretary the "annoyance" Paine and his companions had suffered at their English hotel in Dover shortly before embarking for France.

Paine's contemporaries are authority for the statement that, contrary to the evidence of this letter to Secretary Dundas, "on September 13, 1792, William Blake, the mystical artist and poet, certainly saved Paine from the scaffold by forewarning him that an order had been issued for his arrest."

Incidentally, Thomas Paine is not only depicted by Blake in his illustration of "The spiritual form of Pitt guiding Behemoth," but is mentioned by name in Blake's "Prophecy" concerning America.

I CONCEIVE it necessary to make you acquainted with the following circumstance:—The Department of Calais having elected me a member of the National Convention of France, I set off from London the thirteenth instant, in company with Mr. Frost, of Spring Garden, and Mr. Audibert, one of the municipal officers of Calais, who brought me the certificate of my being elected. We had not arrived more, I believe, than five minutes at the York Hotel, at Dover, when the train of circumstances began that I am going to relate.

We had taken our baggage out of the carriage, and put it into a room, into which we went. Mr. Frost,

179

having occasion to go out, was stopped in the passage by a gentleman, who told him he must return into the room, which he did, and the gentleman came in with him, and shut the door. I had remained in the room; Mr. Audibert was gone to inquire when the packet was to sail. The gentleman then said that he was collector of the customs, and had an information against us, and must examine our baggage for prohibited articles. He produced his commission as collector. Mr. Frost demanded to see the information, which the collector refused to show, and continued to refuse, on every demand that we made. The collector then called in several other officers, and began first to search our pockets. He took from Mr. Audibert, who was then returned into the room, everything he found in his pocket, and laid it on the table. He then searched Mr. Frost in the same manner, (who, among other things, had the keys of the trunks in his pocket,) and then did the same by me.

Mr. Frost wanting to go out, mentioned it, and was going toward the door; on which the collector placed himself against the door, and said, nobody should depart the room. After the keys had been taken from Mr. Frost, (for I had given him the keys of my trunks beforehand, for the purpose of his attending the baggage to the customs, if it should be necessary), the collector asked us to open the trunks, presenting us the keys for that purpose; this we declined to do, unless he would produce his information, which he again refused. The collector then opened the trunks himself, and took out every paper and letter, sealed or unsealed. On our remonstrating with him on the bad policy, as well as the illegality, of Custom House officers seizing papers and letters, which were things that did not came under their cognizance, he replied, that the *Proclamation* gave him the authority.

Among the letters which he took out of my trunk, were two sealed letters, given into my charge by the American Minister in London [Pinckney], one of which was directed to the American Minister at Paris [Gouverneur Morris], the other to a private gentleman; a letter from the President of the United States, and a letter from the Secretary of State in America, both directed to me, and which I had received from the American Minister, now in London, and were private letters of friendship; a letter from the electoral body of the Department of Calais, containing the notification of my being elected to the National Convention; and a letter from the President of the National Assembly, informing me of my being also elected for the Department of the Oise.

As we found that all remonstrances with the collector, on the bad policy and illegality of seizing papers and letters, and retaining our persons by force, under the pretense of searching for prohibited articles, were vain (for he justified himself on the Proclamation, and on the information which he refused to show), we contented ourselves with assuring him, that what he was then doing, he would afterwards have to answer for, and left it to himself to do as he pleased.

It appeared to us that the collector was acting under the direction of some other person or persons, then in the hotel, but whom he did not choose we should see, or who did not choose to be seen by us; for the collector went several times out of the room for a few minutes, and was also called out several times.

When the collector had taken what papers and letters he pleased out of the trunks, he proceeded to read them. The first letter he took up for this purpose was that from the President of the United States to me. While he was doing this, I said, that it was very extraordinary that General Washington could not write a letter of private friendship to me, without its being subject to be read by a Custom House officer. Upon this Mr. Frost laid his hand over the face of the letter, and told the collector that he should not read it, and took it from him. Mr. Frost then, casting his eyes on the concluding paragraph of the letter, said, I will read this part to you, which he did; of which the following is an exact transcript—

And as no one can feel a greater interest in the happiness of mankind than I do, it is the first wish of my heart, that the enlightened policy of the present age may diffuse to all men those blessings to which they are entitled, and lay the foundation of happiness for future generations.

As all the other letters and papers lay then on the table, the collector took them up, and was going out of the room with them. During the transaction already stated, I contented myself with observing what passed, and spoke but little; but on seeing the collector going out of the room with the letters, I told him that the papers and letters then in his hand were either belonging to me, or intrusted to my charge, and that as I could not permit them to be out of my sight, I must insist on going with him.

The collector then made a list of the letters and papers, and went out of the room, giving the letters and papers into the charge of one of the officers. He returned in a short time, and, after some trifling conversation, chiefly about the Proclamation, told us, that he saw *the Proclamation was ill-founded,* and asked if we chose to put the letters and papers into the trunks ourselves, which, as we had not taken them out, we declined doing, and he did it himself, and returned us the keys. In stating to you these matters, I make no complaint against the personal conduct of the collector, or of any of the officers. Their manner was as civil as such an extraordinary piece of business could admit of.

My chief motive in writing to you on this subject is, that you may take measures for preventing the like in future, not only as it concerns private individuals, but in order to prevent a renewal of those unpleasant consequences that have heretofore arisen between nations from circumstances equally as insignificant. I mention this only for myself; but as the interruption extended to two other gentlemen, it is probable that they, as individuals, will take some more effectual mode for redress.

I am, Sir, yours, etc.,

THOMAS PAINE.

P. S. Among the papers seized was a copy of the Attorney-General's information against me for publishing the "Rights of Man" and a printed proof copy of my "Letter to the Addressers," which will soon be published.

LETTER ADDRESSED TO THE ADDRESSERS ON THE LATE PROCLAMATION

PAINE'S "Letter to the Addressers" exhibits his unusual strength of reasoning, supplemented by genuine satire, wit and humor. It was written toward the end of May, 1792, following the Royal Proclamation against seditious writings which was issued on May 21. It was published as a pamphlet, the proof of which Paine took with him from England to France where he read and corrected it for publication in its present form. Its first publishers, or rather co-publishers, were H. D. Symonds, Paternoster Row, and Thomas Clio Rickman, Upper Marylebone Street. Both publishers were eventually prosecuted for their activity in printing and selling the "Rights of Man."

The Proclamation which provoked this letter warns "all our loving subjects, as they tender their own happiness and that of their posterity, to guard against seditious writings which aim at the subversion of all regular government within this kingdom."

COULD I have commanded circumstances with a wish, I know not of any that would have more generally promoted the progress of knowledge, than the late Proclamation, and the numerous rotten borough and corporation addresses thereon. They have not only served as advertisements, but they have excited a spirit of inquiry into the principles of government, and a desire to read the "Rights of Man," in places where that spirit and that work were before unknown.

The people of England, wearied and stunned with parties, and alternately deceived by each, had almost resigned the prerogative of thinking. Even curiosity had expired, and a universal languor had spread itself over the land. The opposition was visibly no other than a contest for power, whilst the mass of the nation stood torpidly by as the prize.

In this hopeless state of things, the first part of the "Rights of Man" made its appearance. It had to combat with a strange mixture of prejudice and indifference; it stood exposed to every species of newspaper abuse; and besides this, it had to remove the obstructions which Mr. Burke's rude and outrageous attack on the French Revolution had artfully raised.

But how easy does even the most illiterate reader distinguish the spontaneous sensations of the heart, from the labored productions of the brain. Truth, whenever it can fully appear, is a thing so naturally familiar to the mind, that an acquaintance commences at first sight. No artificial light, yet discovered, can display all the properties of daylight; so neither can the best invented fiction fill the mind with every conviction which truth begets.

To overthrow Mr. Burke's fallacious book was scarcely the operation of a day. Even the phalanx of placemen and pensioners, who had given the tone to the multitude by clamoring forth his political fame,

became suddenly silent; and the final event to himself
has been, that as he rose like a rocket, he fell like the
stick.

It seldom happens that the mind rests satisfied
with the simple detection of error or imposition.
Once put in motion, *that* motion soon becomes accel-
erated; where it had intended to stop, it discovers new
reasons to proceed, and renews and continues the pursuit far beyond the limits it first prescribed to itself.
Thus it has happened to the people of England. From
a detection of Mr. Burke's incoherent rhapsodies, and
distorted facts, they began an inquiry into the first
principles of government, whilst himself like an
object left far behind, became invisible and forgotten.

Much as the first part of "Rights of Man" impressed at its first appearance, the progressive mind
soon discovered that it did not go far enough. It
detected errors; it exposed absurdities; it shook the
fabric of political superstition; it generated new
ideas; but it did not produce a regular system of
principles in the room of those which it displaced.
And, if I may guess at the mind of the Government-
party, they beheld it as an unexpected gale that would
soon blow over, and they forbore, like sailors in
threatening weather, to whistle, lest they should in-

crease the wind. Everything, on their part, was profound silence.

When the second part of "Rights of Man," *combining Principle and Practise*, was preparing to appear, they affected, for a while, to act with the same policy as before; but finding their silence had no more influence in stifling the progress of the work, than it would have in stopping the progress of time, they changed their plan, and affected to treat it with clamorous contempt. The speech-making placemen and pensioners, and place-expectants, in both Houses of Parliament, the *Outs* as well as the *Ins*, represented it as a silly, insignificant performance; as a work incapable of producing any effect; as something which they were sure the good sense of the people would either despise or indignantly spurn; but such was the overstrained awkwardness with which they harangued and encouraged each other, that in the very act of declaring their confidence they betrayed their fears.

As most of the rotten borough addressers are obscured in holes and corners throughout the country, and to whom a newspaper arrives as rarely as an almanac, they most probably have not had the opportunity of knowing how far this part of the farce (the original prelude to all the addresses) has been

acted.   For *their* information, I will suspend a while
the more serious purpose of my letter, and entertain
them with two or three speeches in the last session of
Parliament, which will serve them for politics till
Parliament meets again.

You must know, gentlemen, that the second part
of the "Rights of Man" (the book against which you
have been presenting addresses, though it is most
probable that many of you did not know it) was to
have come out precisely at the time that Parliament
last met.   It happened not to be published till a few
days after.   But as it was very well known that the
book would shortly appear, the parliamentary orators
entered into a very cordial coalition to cry the book
down, and they began their attack by crying up the
blessings of the Constitution.

Had it been your fate to have been there, you could
not but have been moved at the heart-and-pocket-felt
congratulations that passed between all the parties on
this subject of *blessings;* for the *Outs* enjoy places
and pensions and sinecures as well as the *Ins,* and
are as devoutly attached to the firm of the House.

One of the most conspicuous of this motley group,
is the Clerk of the Court of King's Bench, who calls
himself Lord Stormont.   He is also called Justice
General of Scotland, and Keeper of Scoon (an opposi-

tion man), and he draws from the public for these nominal offices, not less, as I am informed than six thousand pounds a year, and he is, most probably, at the trouble of counting the money and signing a receipt, to show, perhaps, that he is qualified to be clerk as well as justice. He spoke as follows:*

That *we* shall *all* be unanimous in expressing *our* attachment to the Constitution of these realms, *I am confident.* It is a subject upon which there can be *no* divided opinion *in this House.* I do not pretend to be deep read in the knowledge of the Constitution, but *I take upon me* to say, that from the extent of *my* knowledge [*for I have so many thousands a year for nothing*] it appears to *me* that from the period of the Revolution, for it was by no means created then, it has been, both in *theory* and *practise,* the *wisest* system that ever was formed. I never was [he means he never was *till now*] a dealer in *political cant.* My life has not been occupied in *that way,* but the speculations of late years *seem to have taken a turn, for which I cannot account.*

When I came into public life, the political pamphlets of the time, however they might be charged with the heat and violence of parties, were agreed in extolling the radical beauties of the Constitution itself. I remember [*he means he has forgotten*] a most captivating eulogium on its *charms,* by Lord Bolingbroke, where he recommends his readers to contemplate it in all its aspects, with the assurance that it would be found more estimable the more it was *seen.* I do *not recollect* his precise words, but I wish that men who write upon these subjects would take *this for their model,* instead of the political pamphlets, which, I am told, are now in circulation, [such, I suppose, as "Rights of Man,"] pamphlets which I have *not read,* and whose purport

* See his speech in the *Morning Chronicle* of February first. —*Author.*

I know only by *report,* [he means, perhaps, by the *noise* they make].

This, however, I am sure, that pamphlets tending to unsettle the public reverence for the *Constitution,* will have very little influence. They can do very little harm—for [*by the bye, he is no dealer in political cant*] *the English are a sober, thinking people, and are more intelligent, more solid, more steady in their opinions, than any people I ever had the fortune to see.* [This is pretty well laid on, though, for a new beginner.] But if there should ever come a time when the propagation of those doctrines should agitate the public mind, I am *sure* for *every one* of your Lordships, that no attack will be made on the Constitution, from which it is *truly said* that *we* derive *all our* prosperity, without raising *every one* of your Lordships to its support. It will then be found that there is no difference among *us,* but that *we* are *all* determined to *stand* or *fall* together, in defense of the inestimable system [of places and pensions].

After Stormont, on the opposition side, sat down, up rose *another noble Lord,* on the ministerial side, *Grenville.* This man ought to be as strong in the back as a mule, or the *sire* of a mule, or it would crack with the weight of places and offices. He rose, however, without feeling any incumbrance, full master of his weight; and thus said *this* noble Lord to *t'other* noble Lord!

The *patriotic* and *manly* manner in which the noble Lord has declared *his* sentiments on the subject of the Constitution, demands *my* cordial approbation. The noble Viscount has *proved,* that however we may differ on *particular measures,* amidst all the jars and dissonance of *parties,* we are unanimous in *principle.* There is a *perfect and entire consent* [between *us*] in the love and maintenance of the Constitution as *happily subsisting.* It must *undoubtedly* give your Lordships *concern,* to find that the

time is come [heigh ho!] when there is *propriety* in the expressions of regard TO [o! o! o!] THE CONSTITUTION. And that
there are men [confound—their—po-li-tics] who disseminate doctrines *hostile* to the *genuine spirit* of our *well balanced system,*
[it is certainly well balanced when both sides hold places and
pensions at once.] I agree with the noble Viscount that they
have not [I hope] *much success.* I am convinced that there is no
danger to be apprehended from their attempts: but it is *truly*
important and *consolatory* [to us placemen, I suppose] to know,
that if ever there should arise a serious alarm, there is but one
spirit, one sense [and that sense I presume is not *common sense*]
and *one* determination in *this* House [which undoubtedly is to
hold all their places and pensions as long as they can].

Both those speeches (except the parts inclosed in
brackets, which are added for the purpose of *illustration*) are copied *verbatim* from the *Morning Chronicle*
of the first of February last; and when the situation
of the speakers is considered, the one in the Opposition, and the other in the Ministry, and both of them
living at the public expense, by sinecure, or nominal
places and offices, it required a very unblushing front
to be able to deliver them. Can those men seriously
suppose any nation to be so completely blind as not to
see through them? Can Stormont imagine that the
political cant, with which he has larded his harangue,
will conceal the craft? Does he not know that there
never was a cover large enough to hide *itself?* Or
can Grenville believe that his credit with the public
increases with his avarice for places?

But, if these orators will accept a service from me, in return for the allusions they have made to the "Rights of Man," I will make a speech for either of them to deliver, on the excellence of the Constitution, that shall be as much to the purpose as what they have spoken, or as *Bolingbroke's captivating eulogium*. Here it is:

That we shall all be unanimous in expressing our attachment to the Constitution, I am confident. It is, my Lords, incomprehensibly good: but the great wonder of all is the wisdom; for it is, my Lords, *the wisest system that ever was formed*.

With respect to us, noble Lords, though the world does not know it, it is very well known to us, that we have more wisdom than we know what to do with; and what is still better, my Lords, we have it all in stock. I defy your Lordships to prove, that a tittle of it has been used yet; and if we but go on, my Lords, with the frugality we have hitherto done, we shall leave to our heirs and successors, when we go out of the world, the whole stock of wisdom, *untouched*, that we brought in; and there is no doubt but they will follow our example. This, my Lords, is one of the blessed effects of the hereditary system; for we can never be without wisdom so long as we keep it by us, and do not use it.

But, my Lords, as all this wisdom is hereditary property, for the sole benefit of us and our heirs, and it is necessary that the people should know where to get a supply for their own use, the excellence of our Constitution has provided us a king for this very purpose, and for *no other*. But, my Lords, I perceive a defect to which the Constitution is subject, and which I propose to remedy by bringing a bill into Parliament for that purpose.

The Constitution, my Lords, out of delicacy, I presume, has left it as a matter of *choice* to a king whether he will be wise or not. It has not, I mean, my Lords, insisted upon it as a constitutional point, which, I conceive it ought to have done; for I pledge myself to your Lordships to prove, and that with *true patriotic boldness,* that he has *no choice in the matter.* This bill, my Lords, which I shall bring in, will be to declare, that the Constitution, according to the true intent and meaning thereof, does not invest the king with this choice; our ancestors were too wise to do that; and, in order to prevent any doubts that might otherwise arise, I shall prepare, my Lords, an enacting clause, to fix the wisdom of kings by act of Parliament; and then, my Lords, our Constitution will be the wonder of the world!

Wisdom, my Lords, is the one thing needful: but that there may be no mistake in this matter, and that we may proceed consistently with the true wisdom of the Constitution, I shall propose a *certain criterion* whereby the *exact quantity of wisdom* necessary for a king may be known.   [Here should be a cry of, Hear him! Hear him!]

It is recorded, my Lords, in the Statutes at Large of the Jews, a "book, my Lords, which I have not read, and whose purport I know only by report," *but perhaps the bench of Bishops can recollect something about it,* that Saul gave the most convincing proofs of royal wisdom before he was made a king, *for he was sent to seek his father's asses and he could not find them.*

Here, my Lords, we have, most happily for us, a case in point: This precedent ought to be established by act of Parliament; and every king, before he be crowned, should be sent to seek his father's asses, and if he cannot find them, he shall be declared wise enough to be king, according to the true meaning of our excellent Constitution.   All, therefore, my Lords, that will be necessary to be done, by the enacting clause that I shall bring in, will be to invest the king beforehand with the quantity of wisdom necessary for this purpose, lest he should happen not to possess it; and this, my Lords, we can do without making use of any of our own.

We further read, my Lords, in the said Statutes at Large of the Jews, that Samuel, who certainly was as mad as any Man-of-Rights-Man now-a-days (hear him! hear him!), was highly displeased, and even exasperated, at the proposal of the Jews to have a king, and he warned them against it with all that assurance and impudence of which he was master. I have been, my Lords, at the trouble of going all the way to *Paternoster Row*, to procure an extract from the printed copy. I was told that I should meet with it there, or in *Amen-corner*, for I was then going, my Lords, to rummage for it among the curiosities of the *Antiquarian Society*. I will read the extracts to your Lordships, to show how little Samuel knew of the matter.

The extract, my Lords, is from 1 Sam. chap. viii.:

"And Samuel told all the words of the Lord unto the people that asked of him a king.

"And he said, this will be the manner of the king that shall reign over you: he will take your sons, and appoint them for himself, for his chariots, and to be his horsemen; and some shall run before his chariots.

"And he will appoint him captains over thousands, and captains over fifties, and will set them to ear his ground, and to reap his harvest, and to make his instruments of war, and instruments of his chariots.

"And he will take your daughters to be confectionaries, and to be cooks, and to be bakers.

"And he will take your fields, and your vineyards, and your olive-yards, even the best of them, and give them to his servants.

"And he will take the tenth of your seed, and of your vineyards, and give to his officers and to his servants.

"And he will take your man-servants, and your maid-servants, and your goodliest young men, and your asses, and put them to his work.

"And he will take the tenth of your sheep, and ye shall be his servants.

"And ye shall cry out in that day, because of your king, which ye shall have chosen you; and the Lord will not hear you in that day."

Now, my Lords, what can we think of this man, Samuel? Is there a word of truth, or anything like truth, in all that he has said? He pretended to be a prophet, or a wise man, but has not the event proved him to be a fool, or an incendiary?

Look around, my Lords, and see if anything has happened that he pretended to foretell! Has not the most profound peace reigned throughout the world ever since kings were in fashion? Are not, for example, the present kings of Europe the most peaceable of mankind, and the Empress of Russia the very milk of human kindness? It would not be worth having kings, my Lords, if it were not that they never go to war.

If we look at home, my Lords, do we not see the same things here as are seen everywhere else? Are our young men taken to be horsemen, or foot soldiers, any more than in Germany or in Prussia, or in Hanover or in Hesse? Are not our sailors as safe at land as at sea? Are they ever dragged from their homes, like oxen to the slaughter-house, to serve on board ships of war? When they return from the perils of a long voyage with the merchandise of distant countries, does not every man sit down under his own vine and his own fig-tree, in perfect security? Is the tenth of our seed taken by tax-gatherers, or is any part of it given to the King's servants? In short, *is not everything as free from taxes as the light from Heaven!*

Ah! my Lords, do we not see the blessed effect of having kings in everything we look at? Is not the G.R., or the broad R., stamped upon everything? Even the shoes, the gloves, and the hats that we wear, are enriched with the impression, and all our candles blaze a burnt-offering.

Besides these blessings, my Lords, that cover us from the sole of the foot to the crown of the head, do we not see a race of youths growing up to be kings, who are the very paragons of virtue? There is not one of them, my Lords, but might be trusted with untold gold, as safely as the other. Are they not *"more sober, more intelligent, more solid, more steady,"* and withal, more learned, more wise, more everything, than any youths *we "ever had the fortune to see?"* Ah! my Lords, they are a *hopeful family.*

The blessed prospect of succession, which the nation has at this moment before its eyes, is a most undeniable proof of the excellence of our Constitution, and of the blessed hereditary system; for nothing, my Lords, but a constitution founded on the truest and purest wisdom could admit such heaven-born and heaven-taught characters into the government.—Permit me now, my Lords, to recall your attention to the libellous chapter I have just read about kings. I mention this, my Lords, because it is my intention to move for a bill to be brought into Parliament to expunge that chapter from the Bible, and that the Lord Chancellor, with the assistance of the Prince of Wales, the Duke of York, and the Duke of Clarence, be requested to write a chapter in the room of it; and that Mr. Burke do see that it be truly canonical, and faithfully inserted.—*Finis*.

If the clerk of the Court of King's Bench should choose to be the orator of this luminous encomium on the Constitution, I hope he will get it well by heart before he attempts to deliver it, and not have to apologize to Parliament, as he did in the case of Bolingbroke's encomium, for forgetting his lesson; and, with this admonition I leave him.

Having thus informed the Addressers of what passed at the meeting of Parliament, I return to take up the subject at the part where I broke off in order to introduce the preceding speeches.

I was then stating, that the first policy of the Government party was silence, and the next, clamorous contempt; but as people generally choose to read and judge for themselves, the work still went on, and the affectation of contempt, like the silence that preceded it, passed for nothing.

Thus foiled in their second scheme, their evil genius, like a will-with-a-wisp, led them to a third; when all at once, as if it had been unfolded to them by a fortune-teller, or Mr. Dundas had discovered it by second sight, this once harmless, insignificant book, without undergoing the alteration of a single letter, became a most wicked and dangerous libel. The whole Cabinet, like a ship's crew, became alarmed; all hands were piped upon deck, as if a conspiracy of elements was forming around them, and out came the Proclamation and the Prosecution; and addresses supplied the place of prayers.

Ye silly swains, thought I to myself, why do you torment yourselves thus? The "Rights of Man" is a book calmly and rationally written; why then are you so disturbed? Did you see how little or how suspicious such conduct makes you appear, even cunning alone, had you no other faculty, would hush you into prudence. The plans, principles, and arguments, contained in that work, are placed before the eyes of the nation, and of the world, in a fair, open, and manly manner, and nothing more is necessary than to refute them. Do this, and the whole is done; but if ye cannot, so neither can ye suppress the reading, nor convict the author; for the law, in the opinion of

all good men, would convict itself, that should condemn what cannot be refuted.

Having now shown the Addressers the several
stages of the business, prior to their being called
upon, like Cæsar in the Tiber, crying to Cassius,
"help, Cassius, or I sink!" I next come to remark on
the policy of the Government, in promoting addresses; on the consequences naturally resulting
therefrom; and on the conduct of the persons
concerned.

With respect to the policy, it evidently carries with
it every mark and feature of disguised fear. And
it will hereafter be placed in the history of extraordinary things, that a pamphlet should be produced
by an individual, unconnected with any sect or party,
and not seeking to make any, and almost a stranger
in the land, that should completely frighten a whole
government, and that in the midst of its most trium-
phant security. Such a circumstance cannot fail to
prove that either the pamphlet has irresistible powers,
or the Government very extraordinary defects, or
both. The nation exhibits no signs of fear at the
"Rights of Man"; why then should the Government,
unless the interests of the two are really opposite to
each other, and the secret is beginning to be known?
That there are two distinct classes of men in the

nation, those who pay taxes, and those who receive and live upon the taxes, is evident at first sight; and when taxation is carried to excess, it cannot fail to disunite those two, and something of this kind is now beginning to appear.

It is also curious to observe, amidst all the fume and bustle about proclamations and addresses, kept up by a few noisy and interested men, how little the mass of the nation seem to care about either. They appear to me, by the indifference they show, not to believe a word the Proclamation contains; and as to the addresses, they travel to London with the silence of a funeral, and having announced their arrival in the *Gazette,* are deposited with the ashes of their predecessors, and Mr. Dundas writes their *hic jacet.*

One of the best effects which the Proclamation and its echo the addresses have had, has been that of exciting and spreading curiosity; and it requires only a single reflection to discover that the object of all curiosity is knowledge. When the mass of the nation saw that placemen, pensioners, and borough-mongers, were the persons that stood forward to promote addresses, it could not fail to create suspicions that the public good was not their object; that the character of the books, or writings, to which such persons obscurely alluded, not daring to mention them, was directly contrary to what they described them to be, and that it was necessary that every man, for his own satisfaction, should exercise his proper right, and read and judge for himself.

But how will the persons who have been induced to read the "Rights of Man," by the clamor that has been raised against it, be surprised to find, that, instead of a wicked, inflammatory work, instead of a licentious and profligate performance, it abounds with principles of government that are uncontrovertible —with arguments which every reader will feel, are unanswerable—with plans for the increase of commerce and manufactures—for the extinction of war —for the education of the children of the poor—for the comfortable support of the aged and decayed persons of both sexes—for the relief of the army and navy, and, in short, for the promotion of everything that can benefit the moral, civil, and political condition of man.

Why, then, some calm observer will ask, why is the work prosecuted, if these be the goodly matters it contains? I will tell thee, friend; it contains also a plan for the reduction of taxes, for lessening the immense expenses of government, for abolishing sinecure places and pensions; and it proposes applying the redundant taxes, that shall be saved by these reforms, to the purposes mentioned in the former paragraph, instead of applying them to the support of idle and profligate placemen and pensioners.

Is it, then, any wonder that placemen and pensioners, and the whole train of court expectants, should become the promoters of addresses, proclamations, and prosecutions? or, is it any wonder that corporations and rotten boroughs, which are attacked and exposed, both in the first and second parts of "Rights of Man," as unjust monopolies and public nuisances, should join in the cavalcade? Yet these are the sources from which addresses have sprung. Had not such persons come forward to oppose the "Rights of Man," I should have doubted the efficacy of my own writings: but those opposers have now proved to me that the blow was well directed, and they have done it justice by confessing the smart.

The principal deception in this business of addresses has been that the promoters of them have not come forward in their proper characters. They have assumed to pass themselves upon the public as a part of the public, bearing a share of the burden of taxes, and acting for the public good; whereas, they are in general that part of it that adds to the public burden, by living on the produce of the public taxes. They are to the public what the locusts are to the tree: the burden would be less, and the prosperity would be greater, if they were shaken off.

"I do not come here," said Onslow, at the Surrey County meeting, "as the Lord Lieutenant and *Custos Rotulorum* of the county, but I come here as a plain country gentleman." The fact is, that he came as what he was, and as no other, and consequently he came as one of the beings I have been describing. If it be the character of a gentleman to be fed by the public, as a pauper is by the parish, Onslow has a fair claim to the title; and the same description will suit the Duke of Richmond, who led the address at the Sussex meeting. He also may set up for a gentleman.

As to the meeting in the next adjoining county (Kent), it was a scene of disgrace. About two hundred persons met, when a small part of them drew privately away from the rest, and voted an address: the consequence of which was that they got together by the ears, and produced a riot in the very act of producing an address to prevent riots.

That the Proclamation and the addresses have failed of their intended effect, may be collected from the silence which the Government party itself observes. The number of addresses has been weekly retailed in the *Gazette;* but the number of addressers has been concealed. Several of the addresses have been voted by not more than ten or twelve persons; and a considerable number of them by not more than thirty. The whole number of addresses presented at the time of writing this letter is three hundred and twenty, (rotten boroughs and corporations included) and even admitting, on an average, one hundred addressers to each address, the whole number of addressers would be but thirty-two thousand, and nearly three months have been taken up in procuring this number.

That the success of the Proclamation has been less than the success of the work it was intended to discourage, is a matter within my own knowledge; for a greater number of the cheap edition of the first and second parts of the "Rights of Man" has been sold in the space only of one month, than the whole number of addressers (admitting them to be thirty-two thousand) have amounted to in three months.

It is a dangerous attempt in any government to say to a nation, *"thou shalt not read."* This is now done in Spain, and was formerly done under the old government of France; but it served to procure the downfall of the latter, and is subverting that of the former; and it will have the same tendency in all countries; because *thought* by some means or other, is got abroad in the world, and cannot be restrained, though reading may.

If "Rights of Man" were a book that deserved the vile description which promoters of the addresses have given of it, why did not these men prove their charge, and satisfy the people, by producing it, and reading it publicly? This most certainly ought to have been done, and would also have been done, had they believed it would have answered their purpose. But the fact is, that the book contains truths which those timeservers dreaded to hear, and dreaded that the people should know; and it is now following up the addresses in every part of the nation, and convicting them of falsehoods.

Among the unwarrantable proceedings to which the Proclamation has given rise, the meetings of the justices in several of the towns and counties ought to be noticed. Those men have assumed to re-act the farce of general warrants, and to suppress, by their own authority, whatever publications they please. This is an attempt at power equaled only by the conduct of the minor despots of the most despotic governments in Europe, and yet those justices affect to call England a free country. But even this, perhaps, like the scheme for garrisoning the country by building military barracks, is necessary to awaken the country to a sense of its rights, and, as such, it will have a good effect.

Another part of the conduct of such justices has been, that of threatening to take away the licenses from taverns and public-houses, where the inhabitants of the neighborhood associated to read and discuss the principles of government, and to inform each other thereon. This, again, is similar to what is doing in Spain and Russia; and the reflection which it cannot fail to suggest is, that the principles and conduct of any government must be bad, when that government dreads and startles at discussion, and seeks security by a prevention of knowledge.

If the Government, or the Constitution, or by whatever name it be called, be that miracle of perfection which the Proclamation and the addresses have trumpeted it forth to be, it ought to have defied discussion and investigation, instead of dreading it. Whereas, every attempt it makes, either by proclamation, prosecution, or address, to suppress investigation, is a confession that it feels itself unable to bear it. It is error only, and not truth, that shrinks from inquiry. All the numerous pamphlets, and all the newspaper falsehood and abuse, that have been published against the "Rights of Man," have fallen before it like pointless arrows; and, in like manner would any work have fallen before the Constitution, had the Constitution, as it is called, been founded on as good political principles as those on which the "Rights of Man" is written.

It is a good constitution for courtiers, placemen, pensioners, borough-holders, and the leaders of parties, and these are the men that have been the active leaders of addresses; but it is a bad constitution for at least ninety-nine parts of the nation out of an hundred, and this truth is every day making its way.

It is bad, first, because it entails upon the nation the unnecessary expense of supporting three forms and systems of government at once, namely, the monarchical, the aristocratical, and the democratical.

Secondly, because it is impossible to unite such a discordant composition by any other means than perpetual corruption; and therefore the corruption so loudly and so universally complained of, is no other than the natural consequence of such an unnatural compound of governments; and in this consists that excellence which the numerous herd of placemen and pensioners so loudly extol, and which at the same time occasions that enormous load of taxes under which the rest of the nation groans.

Among the mass of national delusions calculated to amuse and impose upon the multitude, the standing one has been that of flattering them into taxes, by calling the Government (or as they please to express it, the English Constitution) *"the envy and the admiration of the world."* Scarcely an address has been voted in which some of the speakers have not uttered this hackneyed, nonsensical falsehood.

Two revolutions have taken place, those of America and France; and both of them have rejected the unnatural compounded system of the English Government. America has declared against all hereditary government, and established the representative system of government only. France has entirely rejected the aristocratical part, and is now discovering the absurdity of the monarchical, and is approaching fast to the representative system. On what ground then, do these men continue a declaration, respecting what they call the *envy and admiration of other nations,* which the voluntary practise of such nations, as have had the opportunity of establishing government, contradicts and falsifies? Will such men never confine themselves to truth? Will they be for ever the deceivers of the people?

But I will go further, and show, that were government now to begin in England, the people could not be brought to establish the same system they now submit to.

In speaking on this subject (or on any other) *on the pure ground of principle,* antiquity and precedent cease to be authority, and hoary-headed error loses its effect. The reasonableness and propriety of things must be examined abstractedly from custom and usage; and, in this point of view, the right which grows into practise today is as much a right, and as old in principle and theory, as if it had the customary sanction of a thousand ages. Principles have no connection with time, nor characters with names.

To say that the Government of this country is composed of Kings, Lords, and Commons, is the mere phraseology of custom. It is composed of men; and whoever the men be to whom the government of any country be intrusted, they ought to be the best and wisest that can be found, and if they are not so, they are not fit for the station. A man derives no more excellence from the change of a name, or calling him king, or calling him lord, than I should do by changing my name from Thomas to George, or from Paine to Guelph. I should not be a whit more able to write a book because my name was altered; neither would any man, now called a king or a lord, have a whit more sense than he now has, were he to call himself Thomas Paine.

As to the word "Commons," applied as it is in England, it is a term of degradation and reproach, and ought to be abolished. It is a term unknown in free countries.

But to the point.—Let us suppose that government was now to begin in England, and that the plan of government, offered to the nation for its approbation or rejection, consisted of the following parts:

First—That some one individual should be taken from all the rest of the nation, and to whom all the rest should swear obedience, and never be permitted to sit down in his presence, and that they should give to him one million sterling a year.—That the nation should never after have power or authority to make laws but with his express consent; and that his sons and his sons' sons, whether wise or foolish, good men or bad, fit or unfit, should have the same power, and also the same money annually paid to them for ever.

Secondly—That there should be two houses of legislators to assist in making laws, one of which should, in the first instance, be entirely appointed by the aforesaid person, and that their sons and their sons' sons, whether wise or foolish, good men or bad, fit or unfit, should for ever after be hereditary legislators.

Thirdly—That the other house should be chosen in the same manner as the house now called the House of Commons is chosen, and should be subject to the control of the two aforesaid hereditary powers in all things.

It would be impossible to cram such a farrago of imposition and absurdity down the throat of this or any other nation that was capable of reasoning upon its rights and its interest.

They would ask, in the first place, on what ground of right, or on what principle, such irrational and preposterous distinctions could, or ought to be made; and what pretensions any man could have, or what services he could render, to entitle him to a million a year? They would go further, and revolt at the idea of consigning their children, and their children's children, to the domination of persons hereafter to be born, who might, for anything they could foresee, turn out to be knaves or fools; and they would finally discover, that the project of hereditary governors and legislators *was a treasonable usurpation over the rights of posterity*. Not only the calm dictates of reason, and the force of natural affection, but the integrity of manly pride, would impel men to spurn such proposals.

From the grosser absurdities of such a scheme, they would extend their examination to the practical defects—They would soon see that it would end in tyranny accomplished by fraud. That in the operation of it, it would be two to one against them, because the two parts that were to be made hereditary would form a common interest, and stick to each other; and that themselves and representatives would become no better than hewers of wood and drawers of water for the other parts of the government.—Yet call one of those powers King, the other Lords, and the third the Commons, and it gives the model of what is called the English Government.

I have asserted, and have shown, both in the first and second parts of "Rights of Man," that there is not such a thing as an English Constitution, and that the people have yet a constitution to form. *A constitution is a thing antecedent to a government; it is the act of a people creating a government and giving it powers, and defining the limits and exercise of the powers so given.* But whenever did the people of England, acting in their original, constituent character, by a delegation elected for that express purpose, declare and say, *"We, the people of this land, do constitute and appoint this to be our system and form of government?"* The government has assumed to constitute itself, but it never was constituted by the people, in whom alone the right of constituting resides.

I will here recite the preamble to the Federal Constitution of the United States of America. I have shown in the second part of "Rights of Man," the manner by which the Constitution was formed and afterwards ratified; and to which I refer the reader. The preamble is in the following words:

WE, THE PEOPLE, of the United States, in order to form a more perfect union, establish justice, insure domestic tranquillity, provide for common defense, promote the general welfare, and secure the blessings of liberty to ourselves and our posterity, DO ORDAIN AND ESTABLISH THIS CONSTITUTION for the United States of America.

Then follow the several articles which appoint the manner in which the several component parts of the government, legislative and executive, shall be elected, and the period of their duration, and the powers they shall have: also, the manner by which future additions, alterations, or amendments, shall be made to the Constitution. Consequently, every improvement that can be made in the science of government, follows in that country as a matter of order. It is only in governments founded on assumption and false principles, that reasoning upon, and investigat-

ing systems and principles of government, and showing their several excellencies and defects, are termed
libellous and seditious.   These terms were made part
of the charge brought against Locke, Hampden, and
Sydney, and will continue to be brought against all
good men, so long as bad government shall continue.

The Government of this country has been ostenta-
tiously giving challenges for more than a hundred
years past, upon what is called its own excellence and
perfection.   Scarcely a king's speech, or a parliamentary speech, has been uttered, in which this glove has
not been thrown, till the world has been insulted with
their challenges.   But it now appears that all this
was vapor and vain boasting, or that it was intended
to conceal abuses and defects, and hush the people
into taxes.

I have taken the challenge up, and in behalf of the
public, have shown, in a fair, open, and candid manner, both the radical and practical defects of the
system; when lo! those champions of the civil list
have fled away, and sent the Attorney-general to deny
the challenge, by turning the acceptance of it into an
attack, and defending their places and pensions by a
prosecution.

I will here drop this part of the subject, and state
a few particulars respecting the prosecution now pend-

ing, by which the Addressers will see that they have been used as tools to the prosecuting party and their dependents. The case is as follows:

The original edition of the first and second bill in the first part of the "Rights of Man"; expensively printed, (in the modern style of printing pamphlets, that they might be bound up with Mr. Burke's "Reflections on the French Revolution,") the high price precluded the generality of people from purchasing; and many applications were made to me from various parts of the country to print the work in a cheaper manner. The people of Sheffield requested leave to print two thousand copies for themselves, with which request I immediately complied.

The same request came to me from Rotherham, from Leicester, from Chester, from several towns in Scotland; and Mr. James Mackintosh, author of "Vindiciæ Gallicæ," brought me a request from Warwickshire, for leave to print ten thousand copies in that county. I had already sent a cheap edition to Scotland; and finding the applications increase, I concluded that the best method of complying therewith, would be to print a very numerous edition in London, under my own direction, by which means the work would be more perfect, and the price be reduced lower than it could be by *printing* small editions in the country, of only a few thousands each.

The cheap edition of the first part was begun about the first of last April, and from that moment, and not before, I expected a prosecution, and the event has proved that I was not mistaken. I had then occasion to write to Mr. Thomas Walker of Manchester, and after informing him of my intention of giving up the work for the purpose of general information, I informed him of what I apprehended would be the consequence; that while the work was at a price that precluded an extensive circulation, the Government party, not able to controvert the plans, arguments, and principles it contained, had chosen to remain silent; but that I expected they would make an attempt to deprive the mass of the nation, and especially the poor, of the right of reading, by the pretense of prosecuting either the author or the publisher, or both. They chose to begin with the publisher.

Nearly a month, however, passed, before I had any information given me of their intentions. I was then at Bromley, in Kent, upon which I came immediately to town, (May 14) and went to Mr. Jordan, the publisher of the original edition. He had that evening been served with a summons to appear at the Court of

King's Bench, on the Monday following, but for what purpose was not stated. Supposing it to be on account of the work, I appointed a meeting with him on the next morning, which was accordingly had, when I provided an attorney, and took the expense of the defense on myself. But finding afterwards that he absented himself from the attorney employed, and had engaged another, and that he had been closeted with the solicitors of the Treasury, I left him to follow his own choice, and he chose to plead guilty.

This he might do if he pleased; and I make no objection against him for it. I believe that his idea by the word *guilty*, was no other than declaring himself to be the publisher, without any regard to the merits or demerits of the work; for were it to be construed otherwise, it would amount to the absurdity of converting a publisher into a jury, and his confession into a verdict upon the work itself. This would be the highest possible refinement upon packing of juries.

On the twenty-first of May, they commenced their prosecution against me, as the author, by leaving a summons at my lodgings in town, to appear at the Court of King's Bench on the eighth of June following; and on the same day, (May 21,) *they issued also their Proclamation*. Thus the Court of St. James and the Court of King's Bench, were playing into each other's hands at the same instant of time, and the farce of addresses brought up the rear; and this mode of proceeding is called by the prostituted name of law. Such a thundering rapidity, after a ministerial dormancy of almost eighteen months, can be attributed to no other cause than their having gained information of the forwardness of the cheap edition, and the dread they felt at the progressive increase of political knowledge.

I was strongly advised by several gentlemen, as well those in the practise of the law, as others, to prefer a bill of indictment against the publisher of the Proclamation, as a publication tending to influence, or rather to dictate the verdict of a jury on the issue of a matter then pending; but it appeared to me much better to avail myself of the opportunity which such a precedent justified me in using, by meeting the Proclamation and the Addressers on their own ground, and publicly defending the work which had been thus unwarrantably attacked and traduced.—And conscious as I now am, that the work entitled "Rights of Man" so far from being, as has been maliciously or erroneously represented, a false, wicked, and seditious libel, is a work abounding with unanswerable truths, with principles of the purest morality and benevo-

lence, and with arguments not to be controverted—
Conscious, I say, of these things, and having no object
in view but the happiness of mankind, I have now put
the matter to the best proof in my power, by giving
to the public a cheap edition of the first and second
parts of that work.

Let every man read and judge for himself, not only
of the merits and demerits of the work, but of the
matters therein contained, which relate to his own
interest and happiness.

If, to expose the fraud and imposition of monarchy,
and every species of hereditary government—to lessen the oppression of taxes—to propose plans for
the education of helpless infancy, and the comfortable support of the aged and distressed—to endeavor
to conciliate nations to each other—to extirpate the
horrid practise of war—to promote universal peace,
civilization, and commerce—and to break the chains
of political superstition, and raise degraded man to
his proper rank;—if these things be libellous, let
me live the life of a libeller, and let the name of
LIBELLER be engraved on my tomb.

Of all the weak and ill-judged measures which fear,
ignorance, or arrogance could suggest, the Proclamation, and the project for addresses, are two of the
worst. They served to advertise the work which the

promoters of those measures wished to keep unknown; and in doing this they offered violence to the judgment of the people, by calling on them to condemn what they forbade them to know, and put the strength of their party to that hazardous issue that prudence would have avoided.—The county meeting for Middlesex was attended by only one hundred and eighteen Addressers. They, no doubt, expected that thousands would flock to their standard, and clamor against the "Rights of Man." But the case most probably is, that men in all countries, are not so blind to their rights and their interest as governments believe.

Having thus shown the extraordinary manner in which the Government party commenced their attack, I proceed to offer a few observations on the prosecution, and on the mode of trial by special jury.

In the first place, I have written a book; and if it cannot be refuted, it cannot be condemned. But I do not consider the prosecution as particularly leveled against me, but against the general right, or the right of every man, of investigating systems and principles of government, and showing their several excellencies or defects. If the press be free only to flatter Government, as Mr. Burke has done, and to cry up and extol what certain Court sycophants are pleased to call a "glorious Constitution," and not free to examine into its errors or abuses, or whether a Constitution really exist or not, such freedom is no other than that of Spain, Turkey, or Russia; and a jury in this case, would not be a jury to try, but an inquisition to condemn.

I have asserted, and by fair and open argument maintained, the right of every nation at all times to establish such a system and form of government for itself as best accords with its disposition, interest, and happiness; and to change and alter it as it sees occasion. Will any jury deny to the nation this right? If they do, they are traitors, and their verdict would be null and void. And if they admit the right, the means must be admitted also; for it would be the highest absurdity to say, that the right existed, but the means did not. The question then is, What are the means by which the possession and exercise of this national right are to be secured? The answer will be, that of maintaining, inviolably, the right of free investigation; for investigation always serves to detect error, and to bring forth truth.

I have, as an individual, given my opinion upon what I believe to be not only the best, but the true system of government, which is the representative system, and I have given reasons for that opinion.

First, Because in the representative system, no office of very extraordinary power, or extravagant pay, is attached to any individual; and consequently there is nothing to excite those national contentions and civil wars with which countries under monarchical governments are frequently convulsed, and of which the history of England exhibits such numerous instances.

Secondly, Because the representative is a system of government always in maturity; whereas monarchical government fluctuates through all the stages, from nonage to dotage.

Thirdly, Because the representative system admits of none but men properly qualified into the government, or removes them if they prove to be otherwise. Whereas, in the hereditary system, a nation may be encumbered with a knave or an idiot for a whole lifetime, and not be benefited by a successor.

Fourthly, Because there does not exist a right to establish hereditary government, or, in other words, hereditary successors, because hereditary government always means a government yet to come, and the case always is, that those who are to live afterwards have the same right to establish government for themselves, as the people had who lived before them; and, therefore, all laws attempting to establish hereditary government, are founded on assumption and political fiction.

If these positions be truths, and I challenge any man to prove the contrary; if they tend to instruct and enlighten mankind, and to free them from error, oppression, and political superstition, which are the objects I have in view in publishing them, that jury would commit an act of injustice to their country, and to me, if not an act of perjury, that should call them *false, wicked,* and *malicious.*

Dragonetti, in his treatise "On Virtues and Rewards," has a paragraph worthy of being recorded in every country in the world—"The science (says he,) of the politician, consists, in fixing the true point of happiness and freedom. Those men deserve the gratitude of ages who should discover a mode of government that contained the greatest sum of *individual happiness* with the least *national expense.*" But if juries are to be made use of to prohibit inquiry, to suppress truth, and to stop the progress of knowledge, this boasted palladium of liberty becomes the most successful instrument of tyranny.

Among the arts practised at the bar, and from the bench, to impose upon the understanding of a jury, and to obtain a verdict where the consciences of men could not otherwise consent, one of the most successful has been that of calling *truth a libel,* and of insinuating that the words *"falsely, wickedly, and maliciously,"* though they are made the formidable and high sounding part of the charge, are not matters of consideration with a jury. For what purpose, then, are they retained, unless it be for that of imposition and wilful defamation?

I cannot conceive a greater violation of order, nor a more abominable insult upon morality, and upon human understanding, than to see a man sitting in the judgment seat, affecting by an antiquated foppery of dress to impress the audience with awe; then causing witnesses and jury to be sworn to truth and justice, himself having officially sworn the same; then causing to be read a prosecution against a man charging him with having *wickedly and maliciously written and published a certain false, wicked, and seditious book;* and having gone through all this with a show of solemnity, as if he saw the eye of the Almighty darting through the roof of the building like a ray of light, turn, in an instant, the whole into a farce, and, in order to obtain a verdict that could not be otherwise obtained, tell the jury that the charge of *falsely, wickedly, and seditiously,* meant nothing; that *truth* was out of the question; and that whether the person accused spoke truth or falsehood, or intended *virtu-*

ously or wickedly, was the same thing; and finally conclude the wretched inquisitorial scene, by stating some antiquated precedent, equally as abominable as that which is then acting, or giving some opinion of his own, and *falsely calling the one and the other* —*Law.* It was, most probably, to such a judge as this, that the most solemn of all reproofs was given— *"The Lord will smite thee, thou whitened wall."* (Paul to Ananias. Acts xxiii. 2.)

I now proceed to offer some remarks on what is called a special jury. As to what is called a special verdict, I shall make no other remark upon it, than that it is in reality *not* a verdict. It is an attempt on the part of the jury to delegate, or of the bench to obtain, the exercise of that right, which is committed to the jury only.

With respect to the special juries, I shall state such matters as I have been able to collect, for I do not find any uniform opinion concerning the mode of appointing them.

In the first place, this mode of trial is but of modern invention, and the origin of it, as I am told, is as follows:

Formerly, when disputes arose between merchants, and were brought before a court, the case was that the nature of their commerce, and the method of keep-

ing merchants' accounts not being sufficiently understood by persons out of their own line, it became necessary to depart from the common mode of appointing
juries, and to select such persons for a jury whose
practical knowledge would enable them to decide
upon the case. From this introduction, special juries
became more general; but some doubts having arisen
as to their legality, an act was passed in the 3d of
George II to establish them as legal, and also to extend them to all cases, not only between individuals,
but in cases where *the Government itself should be
the prosecutor*. This most probably gave rise to the
suspicion so generally entertained of packing a jury;
because, by this act, when the crown, as it is called, is
the prosecutor, the master of the crown-office, who
holds his office under the crown, is the person who
either wholly nominates, or has great power in nominating the jury, and therefore it has greatly the appearance of the prosecuting party selecting a jury.

The process is as follows:

On motion being made in court, by either the
plaintiff or defendant, for a special jury, the court
grants it or not, at its own discretion.

If it be granted, the solicitor of the party that applied for the special jury, gives notice to the solicitor
of the adverse party, and a day and hour are appointed

for them to meet at the office of the master of the crown-office. The master of the crown-office sends to the sheriff or his deputy, who attends with the sheriff's book of freeholders. From this book, forty-eight names are taken, and a copy thereof given to each of the parties; and, on a future day, notice is again given, and the solicitors meet a second time, and each strikes out twelve names. The list being thus reduced from forty-eight to twenty-four, the first twelve that appear in court, and answer to their names, is the special jury for that cause. The first operation, that of taking the forty-eight names, is called nominating the jury; and the reducing them to twenty-four is called striking the jury.

Having thus stated the general process, I come to particulars, and the first question will be, how are the forty-eight names, out of which the jury is to be struck, obtained from the sheriff's book? For herein lies the principal ground of suspicion, with respect to what is understood by packing of juries.

Either they must be taken by some rule agreed upon between the parties, or by some common rule known and established beforehand, or at the discretion of some person, who in such a case, ought to be perfectly disinterested in the issue, as well officially as otherwise.

In the case of merchants, and in all cases between individuals, the master of the office called the crown-office, is officially an indifferent person, and as such may be a proper person to act between the parties, and present them with a list of forty-eight names, out of which each party is to strike twelve. But the case assumes an entire difference of character, when the government itself is the prosecutor. The master of the crown-office is then an officer holding his office under the prosecutor; and it is therefore no wonder that the suspicion of packing juries should, in such cases, have been so prevalent.

This will apply with additional force, when the prosecution is commenced against the author or publisher of such works as treat of reforms, and of the abolition of superfluous places and offices, etc., because in such cases every person holding an office, subject to that suspicion, becomes interested as a party; and the office, called the crown-office, may, upon examination, be found to be of this description.

I have heard it asserted, that the master of the crown-office is to open the sheriff's book as it were per hazard, and take thereout forty-eight *following* names, to which the word merchant or esquire is affixed. The former of these are certainly proper, when the case is between merchants, and it has a reference to the origin of the custom, and to nothing else. As to the word esquire, every man is an esquire who pleases to call himself esquire; and the sensible part of mankind are leaving it off. But the matter for inquiry is, whether there be any existing law to direct the mode by which the forty-eight names shall be taken, or whether the mode be merely that of custom which the office has created; or whether the selection of the forty-eight names be wholly at the discretion and choice of the master of the crown-office? One or other of the two latter appears to be the case, because the act already mentioned, of the 3d of George II lays down no rule or mode, nor refers to any preceding law—but says only, that special juries shall hereafter be struck, *"in such manner as special juries have been and are usually struck."*

This act appears to have been what is generally understood by a *"deep take in."* It was fitted to the spur of the moment in which it was passed, 3d of George II when parties ran high, and it served to throw into the hands of Walpole, who was then Minister, the management of juries in crown prosecutions, by making the nomination of the forty-eight persons, from whom the jury was to be struck, follow the precedent established by custom between individuals, and by this means slipped into practise with less suspicion.

Now, the manner of obtaining special juries through the medium of an officer of the Government, such, for instance, as a master of the crown-office, may be impartial in the case of merchants or other individuals, but it becomes highly improper and suspicious in cases where the Government itself is one of the parties. And it must, upon the whole, appear a strange inconsistency, that a government should keep one officer to commence prosecutions, and another officer to nominate the forty-eight persons from whom the jury is to be struck, both of whom are *officers of the civil list*, and yet continue to call this by the pompous name of *the glorious Right of trial by Jury!*

In the case of the King against Jordan, for publishing the "Rights of Man," the Attorney-general moved for the appointment of a special jury, and the master of the crown-office nominated the forty-eight persons himself, and took them from such part of the sheriff's book as he pleased.

The trial did not come on, occasioned by Jordan withdrawing his plea; but if it had, it might have afforded an opportunity of discussing the subject of special juries; for though such discussion might have had no effect in the Court of King's Bench, it would, in the present disposition for inquiry, have had a considerable effect upon the country; and, in all national reforms, this is the proper point to begin at. Put a country right, and it will soon put government right.

Among the improper things acted by the Government in the case of special juries, on their own motion, one has been that of treating the jury with a dinner, and afterwards giving each juryman two guineas, if a verdict be found for the prosecution, and only one if otherwise; and it has been long observed, that, in London and Westminster, there are persons who appear to make a trade of serving, by being so frequently seen upon special juries.

Thus much for special juries. As to what is called a *common jury*, upon any Government prosecution against the author or publisher of "Rights of Man," during the time of the *present Sheriffry*, I have one question to offer, which is, *whether the present sheriffs of London, having publicly prejudged the case, by the part they have taken in procuring an address from the County of Middlesex, (however diminutive and insignificant the number of Addressers were, being only one hundred and eighteen,) are eligible or proper persons to be intrusted with the power of returning a jury to try the issue of any such prosecution?*

But the whole matter appears, at least to me, to be worthy of a more extensive consideration than what relates to any jury, whether special or common; for the case is, whether any part of a whole nation, locally selected as a jury of twelve men always is, be competent to judge and determine for the whole nation, on any matter that relates to systems and principles of government, and whether it be not applying the institution of juries to purposes for which such institutions were not intended?   For example,

I have asserted in the work, "Rights of Man," that as every man in the nation pays taxes, so has every man a right to a share in government, and consequently that the people of Manchester, Birmingham, Sheffield, Leeds, Halifax, etc., have the same right as those of London.   Shall, then, twelve men, picked out between Templebar and Whitechapel, because the book happened to be first published there, decide upon the rights of the inhabitants of those towns, or of any other town or village in the nation?

Having thus spoken of juries, I come next to offer a few observations on the matter contained in the information or prosecution.

The work, "Rights of Man," consists of part the first, and part the second.   The first part the prosecutor has thought it most proper to let alone; and from the second part he has selected a few short paragraphs, making in the whole not quite two pages of the same printing as in the cheap edition.   Those paragraphs relate chiefly to certain facts, such as the Revolution of 1688, and the coming of George I, commonly called the House of Hanover, or the House of Brunswick, or some such House. The arguments, plans and principles contained in the work, the prosecutor has not ventured to attack. They are beyond his reach.

The act which the prosecutor appears to rest most upon for the support of the prosecution is the act entitled, "An Act, declaring the rights and liberties of the subject, and settling the succession of the Crown," passed in the first year of William and Mary, and more commonly known by the name of the "Bill of Rights."

I have called this bill *"A Bill of wrongs and of insult."* My reasons, and also my proofs, are as follow:

The method and principle which this bill takes for declaring rights and liberties, are in direct contradiction to rights and liberties; it is an assumed attempt to take them wholly from posterity—for the declaration in the said bill is as follows:

"The Lords Spiritual and Temporal, and Commons, do, in *the name of all the people,* most humbly and faithfully *submit themselves, their heirs, and posterity for ever;*" that is, to William and Mary his wife, their heirs and successors. This is a strange way of declaring rights and liberties. But the Parliament who made this declaration in the name, and on the part, of the people, had no authority from them for so doing; and with respect to *posterity for ever*, they had no right or authority whatever in the case. It was assumption and usurpation. I have reasoned very extensively against the principle of this bill the first part of the "Rights of Man"; the prosecutor has silently admitted that reasoning, and he now commences a prosecution on the authority of the bill, after admitting the reasoning against it.

It is also to be observed, that the declaration in this bill, abject and irrational as it is, had no other intentional operation than against the family of the Stuarts, and their abettors. The idea did not then exist, that in the space of an hundred years, posterity might discover a different and much better system of government, and that every species of hereditary government might fall, as popes and monks had fallen before. This I say, was not then thought of, and therefore the application of the bill, in the present case, is a new, erroneous, and illegal application, and is the same as creating a new bill *ex post facto*.

It has ever been the craft of courtiers, for the purpose of keeping up an expensive and enormous civil list, and a mummery of useless and antiquated places and offices at the public expense, to be continually hanging England upon some individual or other, called *King*, though the man might not have capacity to be a parish constable. The folly and absurdity of this is appearing more and more every day; and still those men continue to act as if no alteration in the public opinion had taken place. They hear each other's nonsense, and suppose the whole nation talks the same gibberish.

Let such men cry up the House of Orange, or the House of Brunswick, if they please. They would cry up any other house if it suited their purpose, and give as good reasons for it. But what is this house, or that house, or any other house to a nation? *"For a nation to be free, it is sufficient that she wills it."* Her freedom depends wholly upon herself, and not on any house, nor on any individual. I ask not in what light this cargo of foreign houses appears to others, but I will say in what light it appears to me— it was like the trees of the forest, saying unto the bramble, come thou and reign over us.

Thus much for both their houses. I now come to speak of two other houses, which are also put into the information, and those are the House of Lords, and the House of Commons. Here, I suppose, the Attorney-general intends to prove me guilty of speaking either truth or falsehood; for according to the modern interpretation of libels, it does not signify which, and the only improvement necessary to show the complete absurdity of such doctrine, would be, to prosecute a man for uttering a most *false and wicked truth.*

I will quote the part I am going to give, from the office copy, with the Attorney-general's innuendoes, enclosed in parentheses as they stand in the information, and I hope that civil list officer will caution the court not to laugh when he reads them, and also to take care not to laugh himself.

The information states, that *Thomas Paine, being a wicked, malicious, seditious, and evil-disposed person, hath, with force and arms, and most wicked cunning, written and published a certain false, scandalous, malicious, and seditious libel; in one part thereof, to the tenor and effect following, that is to say—*

With respect to the two Houses, of which the English Parliament (*meaning the Parliament of this Kingdom*) is composed, they appear to be effectually influenced into one, and, as a Legislature, to have no temper of its own. The Minister, (*meaning the Minister employed by the King of this Realm, in the administration of the Government thereof,*) whoever he at any time may be, touches IT (*meaning the two Houses of Parliament of this Kingdom*) as with an opium wand, and IT (*meaning the two Houses of Parliament of this Kingdom*) sleeps obedience.

As I am not malicious enough to disturb their repose, though it be time they should awake, I leave the two Houses and the Attorney-general, to the enjoyment of their dreams, and proceed to a new subject.

The gentlemen, to whom I shall next address myself, are those who have styled themselves *"Friends of the people,"* holding their meetings at the Freemasons' Tavern, London.

One of the principal members of this Society is Mr. Grey, who, I believe, is also one of the most independent members in Parliament. I collect this opinion from what Mr. Burke formerly mentioned to me, rather than from any knowledge of my own. The occasion was as follows:

I was in England at the time the bubble broke forth about Nootka Sound: and the day after the King's Message, as it is called, was sent to Parliament, I wrote a note to Mr. Burke, that upon the condition the French Revolution should not be a subject (for he was then writing the book I have since answered) I would call upon him the next day, and mention some matters I was acquainted with, respecting the affair; for it appeared to me extraordinary that any body of men, calling themselves representatives, should commit themselves so precipitately, or "sleep obedience," as Parliament was then doing, and run a nation into expense, and perhaps a war, without so much as inquiring into the case, or the subject, of both of which I had some knowledge.

When I saw Mr. Burke, and mentioned the circumstances to him, he particularly spoke of Mr. Grey, as the fittest member to bring such matters forward; "for," said Mr. Burke, "*I am not the proper* person to do it, as I am in a treaty with Mr. Pitt about Mr. Hastings's trial." I hope the Attorney-general will allow, that Mr. Burke was then *sleeping his obedience.*—But to return to the Society—

I cannot bring myself to believe, that the general motive of this Society is anything more than that by which every former parliamentary opposition has been governed, and by which the present is sufficiently known. Failing in their pursuit of power and place within doors, they have now (and that in not a very mannerly manner) endeavored to possess themselves of that ground out of doors, which, had it not been made by others, would not have been made by them. They appear to me to have watched, with more cunning than candor, the progress of a certain publication, and when they saw it had excited a spirit of inquiry, and was rapidly spreading, they stepped forward to profit by the opportunity, and Mr. Fox *then* called it a libel.

In saying this, he libelled himself. Politicians of this cast, such, I mean, as those who trim between parties and lie by for events, are to be found in every country, and it never yet happened that they did not do more harm than good. They embarrass business, fritter it to nothing, perplex the people, and the event to themselves generally is, that they go just far enough to make enemies of the few, without going far enough to make friends of the many.

Whoever will read the declarations of this Society, of the twenty-fifth of April and fifth of May, will find a studied reserve upon all the points that are real abuses. They speak not once of the extravagance of government, of the abominable list of unnecessary and sinecure places and pensions, of the enormity of the civil list, of the excess of taxes, nor of any one matter that substantially affects the nation; and from some conversation that has passed in that Society, it does not appear to me that it is any part of their plan to carry this class of reforms into practise. No Opposition party ever did, when it gained possession.

In making these free observations, I mean not to enter into contention with this Society; their incivility toward me is what I should expect from place-hunting reformers. They are welcome, however, to the ground they have advanced upon, and I wish that every individual among them may act in the same upright, uninfluenced, and public-spirited manner that I have done. Whatever reforms may be obtained, and by whatever means, they will be for the benefit of others and not of me. I have no other interest in the cause than the interest of my heart. The part I have acted has been wholly that of a volunteer, unconnected with party; and when I quit, it shall be as honorably as I began.

I consider the reform of Parliament, by an application to Parliament, as proposed by the Society, to be a worn-out, hackneyed subject, about which the nation is tired, and the parties are deceiving each other. It is not a subject that is cognizable before Parliament, because no government has a right to alter itself, either in whole or in part. The right, and the exercise of that right, appertains to the nation only, and the proper means is by a national convention, elected for the purpose, by all the people. By this, the will of the nation, whether to reform or not, or what the reform shall be, or how far it shall extend, will be known, and it cannot be known by any other means. Partial addresses, or separate associations, are not testimonies of the general will.

It is, however, certain that the opinions of men, with respect to systems and principles of government, are changing fast in all countries. The alteration in England, within the space of a little more than a year, is far greater than could have been believed, and it is daily and hourly increasing. It moves along the country with the silence of thought. The enormous expense of government has provoked men to think, by making them feel; and the Proclamation has served to increase jealousy and disgust. To prevent, therefore, those commotions which too often and too suddenly arise from suffocated discontents, it is best that the general WILL should have the full and free opportunity of being publicly ascertained and known.

Wretched as the state of representation is in England, it is every day becoming worse, because the unrepresented parts of the nation are increasing in population and property, and the represented parts are decreasing. It is, therefore, no ill-grounded estimation to say that as not one person in seven is represented, at least fourteen millions of taxes out of the seventeen millions, are paid by the unrepresented part; for although copyholds and leaseholds are assessed to the land-tax the holders are unrepresented. Should then a general demur take place as to the obligation of paying taxes, on the ground of not being represented, it is not the representatives of rotten boroughs, nor special juries, that can decide the question. This is one of the possible cases that ought to be foreseen, in order to prevent the inconveniences that might arise to numerous individuals, by provoking it.

I confess I have no idea of petitioning for rights. Whatever the rights of people are, they have a right to them, and none have a right either to withhold them, or to grant them. Government ought to be established on such principles of justice as to exclude the occasion of all such applications, for wherever they appear they are virtually accusations.

I wish that Mr. Grey, since he has embarked in the business, would take the whole of it into consideration. He will then see that the right of reforming the state of the representation does not reside in Parliament, and that the only motion he could consistently make would be, that Parliament should *recommend* the election of a convention of the people, because all pay taxes. But whether Parliament recommended it or not, the right of the nation would neither be lessened nor increased thereby.

As to petitions from the unrepresented part, they ought not to be looked for. As well might it be expected that Manchester, Sheffield, etc., should petition the rotten boroughs, as that they should petition the representatives of those boroughs. Those two towns alone pay far more taxes than all the rotten boroughs put together, and it is scarcely to be expected they should pay their court either to the boroughs, or the borough-mongers.

It ought also to be observed, that what is called Parliament, is composed of two Houses that have always declared against the right of each other to interfere in any matter that related to the circumstances of either, particularly that of election. A reform, therefore, in the representation cannot, on the ground they have individually taken, become the subject of an act of Parliament, because such a mode would include the interference, against which the Commons on their part have protested; but must, as well on the ground of formality, as on that of right, proceed from a national convention.

Let Mr. Grey, or any other man, sit down and endeavor to put his thoughts together, for the purpose of drawing up an application to Parliament for a reform of Parliament, and he will soon convince himself of the folly of the attempt. He will find that he cannot get on; that he cannot make his thoughts join, so as to produce any effect; for, whatever formality of words he may use, they will unavoidably include two ideas directly opposed to each other; the one in setting forth the reasons, the other in praying for relief, and the two, when placed together, would stand thus: *"The representation in Parliament is so very corrupt, that we can no longer confide in it,—and, therefore, confiding in the justice and wisdom of Parliament, we pray,"* etc., etc.

The heavy manner in which every former proposed application to Parliament has dragged, sufficiently shows, that though the nation might not exactly see the awkwardness of the measure, it could not clearly see its way, by those means. To this also may be added another remark, which is, that the worse Parliament is, the less will be the inclination to petition it. This indifference, viewed as it ought to be, is one of the strongest censures the public express. It is as if they were to say to them, "Ye are not worth reforming."

Let any man examine the Court-calendar of placemen in both houses, and the manner in which the civil list operates, and he will be at no loss to account for this indifference and want of confidence on one side, nor of the opposition to reforms on the other.

Who would have supposed that Mr. Burke, holding forth as he formerly did against secret influence, and corrupt majorities, should become a concealed pensioner? I will now state the case, not for the little purpose of exposing Mr. Burke, but to show the inconsistency of any application to a body of men, more than half of whom, as far as the nation can at present know, may be in the same case with himself.

Toward the end of Lord North's administration, Mr. Burke brought a bill into Parliament, generally known as Mr. Burke's Reform Bill; in which, among other things, it is enacted, "That no pension exceeding the sum of three hundred pounds a year, shall be granted to any one person, and that the whole amount of the pensions granted in one year shall not exceed six hundred pounds; a list of which, together with the *names of the persons* to whom the same are granted, shall be laid before Parliament in twenty days after the beginning of each session, until the whole pension list shall be reduced to ninety thousand pounds." A provisory clause is afterwards added, "That it shall be lawful for the First Commissioner of the Treasury, to return into the Exchequer any pension or annuity, *without a name,* on his making oath that such pension or annuity is not directly or indirectly for the benefit, use, or behoof of any member of the House of Commons."

But soon after that administration ended, and the party Mr. Burke acted with came into power, it appears from the circumstances I am going to relate, that Mr. Burke became himself a pensioner in disguise; in a similar manner as if a pension had been granted in the name of John Nokes, to be privately paid to and enjoyed by Tom Stiles. The name of Edmund Burke does not appear in the original transaction: but after the pension was obtained, Mr. Burke wanted to make the most of it at once, by selling or mortgaging it; and the gentleman in whose name the pension stands, applied to one of the public offices for that purpose. This unfortunately brought forth the name of *Edmund Burke,* as the real pensioner of £1,500 per annum. When men trumpet forth what they call the blessings of the Constitution, it ought to be known what sort of blessings they allude to.

As to the civil list of a million a year, it is not to be supposed that any one man can eat, drink, or consume the whole upon himself. The case is, that above half the sum is annually apportioned among courtiers, and court members, of both houses, in places and offices, altogether insignificant and perfectly useless as to every purpose of civil, rational, and manly government. For instance:

Of what use in the science and system of government is what is called a lord chamberlain, a master and mistress of the robes, a master of the horse, a master of the hawks, and one hundred other such things? Laws derive no additional force, nor additional excellence from such mummery.

In the disbursements of the civil list for the year 1786, (which may be seen in Sir John Sinclair's "History of the Revenue,") are four separate charges for this mummery office of chamberlain:

1st, ... 38,778*l*. 17*s*.	—
2d, ... 3,000	—	—
3d, ... 24,069	19	—
4th, ... 10,000	18	3*d*.

75,849*l*. 14*s*.   3*d*.

Besides £1,119 charged for alms.

From this sample the rest may be guessed at. As to the master of the hawks, (there are no hawks kept, and if there were, it is no reason the people should pay the expense of feeding them, many of whom are put to it to get bread for their children,) his salary is £1,372 10s.

And besides a list of items of this kind, sufficient to fill a quire of paper, the pension lists alone are £107,404 13*s*. 4*d*. which is a greater sum than all the expenses of the Federal Government of America.

Among the items, there are two I had no expectation of finding, and which, in this day of inquiry after civil list influence, ought to be exposed. The one is an annual payment of one thousand seven hundred pounds to the dissenting ministers in England, and the other, eight hundred pounds to those of Ireland.

This is the fact; and the distribution, *as I am informed*, is as follows: The whole sum of £1,700 is paid to one person, a dissenting minister in London, who divides it among eight others, and those eight among such others as they please. The lay-body of the dissenters, and many of their principal ministers, have long considered it as dishonorable, and have endeavored to prevent it, but still it continues to be secretly paid; and as the world has sometimes seen very fulsome addresses from parts of that body, it may naturally be supposed that the receivers, like bishops and other court-clergy, are not idle in promoting them. How the money is distributed in Ireland, I know not.

To recount all the secret history of the civil list, is not the intention of this publication. It is sufficient, in this place, to expose its general character, and the mass of influence it keeps alive. It will necessarily become one of the objects of reform; and therefore enough is said to show that, under its operation, no application to Parliament can be expected to succeed, nor can consistently be made.

July 14, 1789

From a contemporary engraving.

The famous prison is shown at the left. The Governor's Mansion at the right is in flames. In the right foreground Governor de Launey is being taken prisoner by a grenadier and a civilian. He was torn to pieces by the mob, and his head carried on a pike through the streets of Paris. Paris was still jubilant over the fall of the Bastille when Thomas Paine arrived in the city to take a prominent place among the leaders of the French Revolution.

Fall of the Bastille

July 14, 1789

From a contemporary engraving.

The famous prison is shown at the left. The Governor's Mansion at the right is in flames. In the right foreground Governor de Launey is being taken prisoner by a grenadier and a civilian. He was torn to pieces by the mob, and his head carried on a pike through the streets of Paris. Paris was still jubilant over the fall of the Bastille when Thomas Paine arrived in the city to take a prominent place among the leaders of the French Revolution.

Such reforms will not be promoted by the party that is in possession of those places, nor by the opposition who are waiting for them; and as to a *mere reform,* in the state of the representation, the idea that another Parliament, differently elected from the present, but still a third component part of the same system, and subject to the control of the other two parts, will abolish those abuses, is altogether delusion; because it is not only impracticable on the ground of formality, but is unwisely exposing another set of men to the same corruptions that have tainted the present.

Were all the objects that require reform accomplishable by a mere reform in the state of representation, the persons who compose the present Parliament might, with rather more propriety, be asked to abolish all the abuses themselves, than be applied to as the mere instruments of doing it by a future Parliament. If the virtue be wanting to abolish the abuse, it is also wanting to act as the means, and the nation must, from necessity, proceed by some other plan.

Having thus endeavored to show what the abject condition of Parliament is, and the impropriety of going a second time over the same ground that has before miscarried, I come to the remaining part of the subject.

There ought to be, in the constitution of every country, a mode of referring back, on any extraordinary occasion, to the sovereign and original constituent power, which is the nation itself. The right of altering any part of a government, cannot, as already observed, reside in the government, or that government might make itself what it pleased.

It ought also to be taken for granted, that though a nation may feel inconveniences, either in the excess of taxation, or in the mode of expenditure, or in anything else, it may not at first be sufficiently assured in what part of its government the defect lies, or where the evil originates. It may be supposed to be in one part, and on inquiry be found to be in another; or partly in all. This obscurity is naturally interwoven with what are called mixed governments.

Be, however, the reform to be accomplished whatever it may, it can only follow in consequence of obtaining a full knowledge of all the causes that have rendered such reform necessary, and everything short of this is guess-work or frivolous cunning. In this case, it cannot be supposed that any application to Parliament can bring forward this knowledge. That body is itself the supposed cause, or one of the supposed causes, of the abuses in question; and cannot be expected, and ought not to be asked, to give evidence against itself. The inquiry, therefore, which is of necessity the first step in the business, cannot be trusted to Parliament, but must be undertaken by a distinct body of men, separated from every suspicion of corruption or influence.

Instead, then, of referring to rotten boroughs and absurd corporations for addresses, or hawking them about the country to be signed by a few dependent tenants, the real and effectual mode would be to come at once to the point, and ascertain the sense of the nation by electing a national convention. By this method, as already observed, the general WILL, whether to reform or not, or what the reform shall be, or how far it shall extend, will be known, and it cannot be known by any other means.

Such a body, empowered and supported by the nation, will have authority to demand information upon all matters necessary to be inquired into; and no minister, nor any person, will dare to refuse it. It will then be seen whether seventeen millions of taxes are necessary, and for what purposes they are expended. The concealed pensioners will then be obliged to unmask; and the source of influence and corruption, if any such there be, will be laid open to the nation, not for the purpose of revenge, but of redress.

By taking this public and national ground, all objections against partial addresses on the one side, or private associations on the other, will be done away; THE NATION WILL DECLARE ITS OWN REFORMS; and the clamor about party and faction, or ins or outs, will become ridiculous.

The plan and organization of a convention is easy in practise.

In the first place, the number of inhabitants in every county can be sufficiently ascertained from the number of houses assessed to the house and window-light tax in each county. This will give the rule for apportioning the number of members to be elected to the national convention in each of the counties.

If the total number of inhabitants in England be seven millions and the total number of members to be elected to the convention be one thousand, the number of members to be elected in a county containing one hundred and fifty thousand inhabitants will be *twenty-one,* and in like proportion for any other county.

As the election of a convention must, in order to ascertain the general sense of the nation, go on grounds different from that of parliamentary elections, the mode that best promises this end will have no difficulties to combat with from absurd customs and pretended rights. The right of every man will be the same, whether he lives in a city, a town, or a village. The custom of attaching rights to *place*, or in other words, to inanimate matter, instead of to the *person*, independently of place, is too absurd to make any part of a rational argument.

As every man in the nation, of the age of twenty-one years, pays taxes, either out of the property he possesses, or out of the product of his labor, which is property to him; and is amenable in his own person to every law of the land; so has everyone the same equal right to vote, and no one part of the nation, nor any individual, has a right to dispute the right of another. The man who should do this ought to forfeit the exercise of his *own* right, for a term of years. This would render the punishment consistent with the crime.

When a qualification to vote is regulated by years, it is placed on the firmest possible ground; because the qualification is such, as nothing but dying before the time can take away; and the equality of rights, as a principle, is recognized in the act of regulating the exercise. But when rights are placed upon, or made dependent upon property, they are on the most precarious of all tenures. "Riches make themselves wings, and fly away," and the rights fly with them; and thus they become lost to the man when they would be of most value.

It is from a strange mixture of tyranny and cowardice, that exclusions have been set up and continued. The boldness to do wrong at first, changes afterwards into cowardly craft, and at last into fear. The representatives in England appear now to act as if they were afraid to do right, even in part, lest it should awaken the nation to a sense of all the wrongs it has endured. This case serves to show that the same conduct that best constitutes the safety of an individual, namely, a strict adherence to principle, constitutes also the safety of a government, and that without it safety is but an empty name. When the rich plunder the poor of his rights, it becomes an example to the poor to plunder the rich of his property; for the rights of the one are as much property to him, as wealth is property to the other, and the *little all* is as dear as the *much*. It is only by setting out on just principles that men are trained to be just to each other; and it will always be found, that when the rich protect the rights of the poor, the poor will protect the property of the rich. But the guarantee, to be effectual, must be parliamentarily reciprocal.

Exclusions are not only unjust, but they frequently operate as injuriously to the party who monopolizes, as to those who are excluded. When men seek to exclude others from participating in the exercise of any right, they should at least, be assured, that they can effectually perform the whole of the business they undertake; for, unless they do this, themselves will be losers by the monopoly. This has been the case with respect to the monopolized right of election. The monopolizing party has not been able to keep the Parliamentary representation, to whom the power of taxation was intrusted, in the state it ought to have been, and have thereby multiplied taxes upon themselves equally with those who were excluded.

A great deal has been, and will continue to be said, about disqualifications, arising from the commission of offenses; but were this subject urged to its full extent, it would disqualify a great number of the present electors, together with their representatives; for, of all offenses, none are more destructive to the morals of society than bribery and corruption. It is, therefore, civility to such persons to pass this subject over, and give them a fair opportunity of recovering, or rather of creating character.

Everything, in the present mode of electioneering in England, is the reverse of what it ought to be, and the vulgarity that attends elections is no other than the natural consequence of inverting the order of the system.

In the first place, the candidate seeks the elector, instead of the elector seeking for a representative; and the electors are advertised as being in the interest of the candidate, instead of the candidate being in the interest of the electors. The candidate pays the elector for his vote, instead of the nation paying the representative for his time and attendance on public business. The complaint for an undue election is brought by the candidate, as if he, and not the electors, were the party aggrieved; and he takes on himself, at any period of the election, to break it up, by declining, as if the election was in his right and not in theirs.

The compact that was entered into at the last Westminster election between two of the candidates (Mr. Fox and Lord Hood,) was an indecent violation of the principles of election. The candidates assumed, in their own persons, the rights of the electors; for, it was only in the body of the electors, and not at all in the candidates, that the right of making such compact, or compromise, could exist. But the principle of election and representation is so completely done away in every stage thereof, that inconsistency has no longer the power of surprising.

Neither from elections thus conducted, nor from rotten borough addressers, nor from county-meetings, promoted by placemen and pensioners, can the sense of the nation be known. It is still corruption appealing to itself. But a convention of a thousand persons, fairly elected, would bring every matter to a decided issue.

As to county-meetings, it is only persons of leisure, or those who live near to the place of meeting, that can attend, and the number on such occasions is but like a drop in the bucket compared with the whole. The only consistent service which such meetings could render, would be that of apportioning the county into convenient districts, and when this is done, each district might, according to its number of inhabitants, elect its quota of county members to the national convention; and the vote of each elector might be taken in the parish where he resided, either by ballot or by voice, as he should choose to give it.

A national convention thus formed, would bring together the sense and opinions of every part of the nation, fairly taken. The science of government, and the interest of the public, and of the several parts thereof, would then undergo an ample and rational discussion, freed from the language of parliamentary disguise.

But in all deliberations of this kind, though men have a right to reason with, and endeavor to convince each other, upon any matter that respects their common good, yet, in point of practise, the majority of opinions, when known, forms a rule for the whole, and to this rule every good citizen practically conforms.

Mr. Burke, as if he knew (for every concealed pensioner has the opportunity of knowing,) that the abuses acted under the present system, are too flagrant to be palliated, and that the majority of opinions, whenever such abuses should be made public, would be for a general and effectual reform, has endeavored to preclude the event, by sturdily denying the right of a majority of a nation to act as a whole. Let us bestow a thought upon this case.

When any matter is proposed as a subject for consultation, it necessarily implies some mode of decision. Common consent, arising from absolute necessity, has placed this in a majority of opinions; because, without it, there can be no decision, and consequently no order. It is, perhaps, the only case in which mankind, however various in their ideas upon other matters, can consistently be unanimous;

because it is a mode of decision derived from the primary original right of every individual concerned; *that* right being first individually exercised in giving an opinion, and whether that opinion shall arrange with the minority or the majority, is a subsequent accidental thing that neither increases nor diminishes the individual, original right itself. Prior to any debate, inquiry, or investigation, it is not supposed to be known on which side the majority of opinions will fall, and therefore, while this mode of decision secures to everyone the right of giving an opinion, it admits to everyone an equal chance in the ultimate event.

Among the matters that will present themselves to the consideration of a national convention, there is one, wholly of a domestic nature, but so marvellously loaded with confusion, as to appear at first sight, almost impossible to be reformed. I mean the condition of what is called law.

But, if we examine into the cause from whence this confusion, now so much the subject of universal complaint, is produced, not only the remedy will immediately present itself, but, with it, the means of preventing the like case hereafter.

In the first place, the confusion has generated itself from the absurdity of every Parliament assuming to be eternal in power, and the laws partake in a similar manner, of this assumption. They have no period of legal or natural expiration; and, however absurd in principle, or inconsistent in practise many of them have become, they still are, if not especially repealed, considered as making a part of the general mass. By this means the body of what is called law, is spread over a space of *several hundred years,* comprehending laws obsolete, laws repugnant, laws ridiculous, and every other kind of laws forgotten or remembered; and what renders the case still worse, is, that the confusion multiplies with the progress of time.*

To bring this misshapen monster into form, and to prevent its lapsing again into a wilderness state, only two things, and those very simple, are necessary.

The first is, to review the whole mass of laws, and to bring forward such only as are worth retaining, and let all the rest drop; and to give to the laws so brought forward a new era, commencing from the time of such reform.

* In the time of Henry IV a law was passed making it felony "to multiply gold or silver, or to make use of the craft of multiplication," and this law remained two hundred and eighty-six years upon the statute books. It was then repealed as being ridiculous and injurious.—*Author.*

Secondly; that at the expiration of every twenty-one years (or any other stated period) a like review shall again be taken, and the laws, found proper to be retained, be again carried forward, commencing with that date, and the useless laws dropped and discontinued.

By this means there can be no obsolete laws, and scarcely such a thing as laws standing in direct or equivocal contradiction to each other, and every person will know the period of time to which he is to look back for all the laws in being.

It is worth remarking, that while every other branch of science is brought within some commodious system, and the study of it simplified by easy methods, the laws take the contrary course, and become every year more complicated, entangled, confused, and obscure.

Among the paragraphs which the Attorney-general has taken from the "Rights of Man," and put into his information, one is, that where I have said, "that with respect to regular law, there is *scarcely such a thing*."

As I do not know whether the Attorney-general means to show this expression to be libellous, because it is TRUE, or because it is FALSE, I shall make no other reply to him in this place, than by remarking, that if almanac-makers had not been more judicious than law-makers, the study of almanacs would by this time have become as abstruse as the study of law, and we should hear of a library of almanacs as we now do of statutes; but by the simple operation of letting the obsolete matter drop, and carrying forward that only which is proper to be retained, all that is necessary to be known is found within the space of a year, and laws also admit of being kept within some given period.

I shall here close this letter, so far as it respects the addresses, the Proclamation, and the prosecution; and shall offer a few observations to the Society, styling itself "THE FRIENDS OF THE PEOPLE."

That the science of government is beginning to be better understood than in former times, and that the age of fiction and political superstition, and of craft and mystery, is passing away, are matters which the experience of every day proves to be true, as well in England as in other countries.

As therefore it is impossible to calculate the silent progress of opinion, and also impossible to govern a nation after it has changed its habits of thinking, by the craft or policy that it was governed by before, the only true method to prevent popular discontents and commotions is, to throw, by every fair and rational argument, all the light upon the subject than can possibly be thrown; and at the same time, to open the means of collecting the general sense of the nation; and this cannot, as already observed, be done by any plan so effectually as a national convention. Here individual opinion will quiet itself by having a center to rest upon.

The Society already mentioned, (which is made up of men of various descriptions, but chiefly of those called Foxites,) appears to me, either to have taken wrong grounds from want of judgment, or to have acted with cunning reserve. It is now amusing the people with a new phrase, namely, that of "a temperate and moderate reform," the interpretation of which is, *a continuance of the abuses as long as possible. If we cannot hold all let us hold some.*

Who are those that are frightened at reforms? Are the public afraid that their taxes should be lessened too much? Are they afraid that sinecure places and pensions should be abolished too fast? Are the poor afraid that their condition should be rendered too comfortable? Is the worn-out mechanic, or the aged and decayed tradesman, frightened at the prospect of receiving ten pounds a year out of the surplus taxes? Is the soldier frightened at the thoughts of his discharge, and three shillings per week during life? Is the sailor afraid that press-warrants will be abolished? The Society mistakes the fears of borough mongers, placemen, and pensioners, for the fears of the people; and the *temperate and moderate reform* it talks of is calculated to suit the condition of the former.

Those words, "temperate and moderate," are words either of political cowardice, or of cunning, or seduction.—A thing, moderately good, is not so good as it ought to be. Moderation in temper is always a virtue; but moderation in principle, is a species of vice. But who is to be the judge of what is a temperate and moderate reform? The Society is the representative of nobody; neither can the unrepresented part of the nation commit this power to those in Parliament, in whose election they had no choice; and, therefore, even, upon the ground the Society has taken, recourse must be had to a national convention.

The objection which Mr. Fox made to Mr. Grey's proposed motion for a parliamentary reform was, that it contained no plan.—It certainly did not. But the plan very easily presents itself; and while it is fair for all parties, it prevents the dangers that might otherwise arise from private or popular discontent.

THOMAS PAINE.

ADDRESS TO THE PEOPLE OF FRANCE

THE French National Assembly, on August 26, 1792, had voted the title of citizen to Paine, along with Washington, Hamilton, Madison and a number of European liberal leaders such as Bentham, Wilberforce, Klopstock and Kosciusko. This address in acknowledgment of the honor was made on September 25 of "the first year of the Republic."

Several departments had elected Paine as their deputy to the French Convention, and on his arrival from England he had accepted the election of Pas-de-Calais, and attended the sessions of the Convention.

Had Napoleon remembered and considered one paragraph of this address he might never have led his army on the disastrous march to Moscow in 1812. It reads: "Were it now to be proposed to the Austrians and Prussians [with whom France was then at war] to escort them into the middle of France, and there leave them to make the most of such a situation, they would see too much into the dangers of it to accept the offer."

FELLOW CITIZENS,

I receive, with affectionate gratitude, the honor which the late National Assembly has conferred upon me, by adopting me a citizen of France: and the additional honor of being elected by my fellow citizens a member of the National Convention. Happily impressed, as I am, by those testimonies of respect shown toward me as an individual, I feel my felicity increased by seeing the barrier broken down that divided patriotism by spots of earth, and limited citizenship to the soil, like vegetation. Had those honors been conferred in an hour of national tranquillity, they

265

would have afforded no other means of showing my affection, than to have accepted and enjoyed them; but they come accompanied with circumstances that give me the honorable opportunity of commencing my citizenship in the stormy hour of difficulties. I come not to enjoy repose. Convinced that the cause of France is the cause of all mankind, and that liberty cannot be purchased by a wish, I gladly share with you the dangers and honors necessary to success.

I am well aware that the moment of any great change, such as that accomplished on the tenth of August, is unavoidably the moment of terror and confusion. The mind, highly agitated by hope, suspicion and apprehension, continues without rest till the change be accomplished. But let us now look calmly and confidently forward, and success is certain. It is no longer the paltry cause of kings, or of this, or of that individual, that calls France and her armies into action. It is the great cause of ALL. It is the establishment of a new era, that shall blot despotism from the earth, and fix, on the lasting principles of peace and citizenship, the great Republic of Man.

It has been my fate to have borne a share in the commencement and complete establishment of one revolution (I mean the Revolution of America). The success and events of that revolution are encouraging to us.   The prosperity and happiness that have since flowed to that country, have amply rewarded her for all the hardships she endured and for all the dangers she encountered.

The principles on which that Revolution began, have extended themselves to Europe; and an over-ruling Providence is regenerating the old world by the principles of the new.   The distance of America from all the other parts of the globe, did not admit of her carrying those principles beyond her own sit-uation.   It is to the peculiar honor of France, that she now raises the standard of liberty for all nations; and in fighting her own battles, contends for the rights of all mankind.

The same spirit of fortitude that insured success to America will insure it to France, for it is impos-sible to conquer a nation determined to be free!   The military circumstances that now unite themselves to France are such as the despots of the earth know nothing of, and can form no calculation upon.   They know not what it is to fight against a nation; they have only been accustomed to make war upon each other, and they know, from system and practise, how to calculate the probable success of despot against despot; and here their knowledge and their experience end.

But in a contest like the present a new and boundless variety of circumstances arise, that derange all such customary calculations. When a whole nation acts as an army, the despot knows not the extent of the power against which he contends. New armies arise against him with the necessity of the moment. It is then that the difficulties of an invading enemy multiply, as in the former case they diminished; and he finds them at their height when he expected them to end.

The only war that has any similarity of circumstances with the present, is the late Revolution War in America. On her part, as it now is in France, it was a war of the whole nation:—there it was that the enemy, by beginning to conquer, put himself in a condition of being conquered. His first victories prepared him for defeat. He advanced till he could not retreat, and found himself in the midst of a nation of armies.

Were it now to be proposed to the Austrians and Prussians, to escort them into the middle of France, and there leave them to make the most of such a situation, they would see too much into the dangers of it to accept the offer, and the same dangers would attend them, could they arrive there by any other means. Where, then, is the military policy of their attempting to obtain, by force, that which they would refuse by choice? But to reason with despots is throwing reason away. The best of arguments is a vigorous preparation.

Man is ever a stranger to the ways by which Providence regulates the order of things. The interfer-ence of foreign despots may serve to introduce into their own enslaved countries the principles they come to oppose. Liberty and equality are blessings too great to be the inheritance of France alone. It is an honor to her to be their first champion; and she may now say to her enemies, with a mighty voice, "O! ye Austrians, ye Prussians! ye who now turn your bayonets against us, it is for you, it is for all Europe, it is for all mankind, and not for France alone, that she raises the standard of Liberty and Equality!"

The public cause has hitherto suffered from the contradictions contained in the Constitution of the Constituent Assembly. Those contradictions have served to divide the opinions of individuals at home, and to obscure the great principles of the Revolution in other countries. But when those contradictions shall be removed, and the Constitution be made con-formable to the Declaration of Rights; when the bagatelles of monarchy, royalty, regency and hereditary succession, shall be exposed, with all their absurdities, a new ray of light will be thrown over the world, and the Revolution will derive new strength by being universally understood.

The scene that now opens itself to France extends far beyond the boundaries of her own dominions. Every nation is becoming her colleague, and every court is become her enemy. It is now the cause of all nations, against the cause of all courts. The terror that despotism felt, clandestinely begot a confederation of despots; and their attack upon France was produced by their fears at home.

In entering on this great scene, greater than any nation has yet been called to act in let us say to the agitated mind, be calm. Let us punish by instructing, rather than by revenge. Let us begin the new era by a greatness of friendship, and hail the approach of union and success.

Your fellow-citizen,
THOMAS PAINE.

AN ESSAY FOR THE USE OF NEW REPUBLICANS IN THEIR OPPOSITION TO MONARCHY

THIS article first appeared in "Le Patriote François" of October 20, 1792. In it Paine occasionally repeats a sentence or a paragraph from his earlier writings, and re-presents his well-known anti-royalist principles.

Assembling on September 21, 1792, the National Convention first took steps to abolish Royalty, and the next day established the revolutionary calendar. A few days after making public this essay Paine was delegated to felicitate the Convention, which he did in these words freely translated: "Citizen President: In behalf of my fellow-deputies and of the General Council of the Commune of Calais I have the honor of congratulating the Convention on the abolition of Royalty. At the same time, I must, in the midst of the popular rejoicing, express my regret that the folly of our ancestors should compel us to treat with such solemnity the laying of a phantom."

THE attainment of any important possession that we have long been ardently coveting is at once a source of subsequent self-congratulation. Indeed, the feeling that we have triumphed so absorbs us that we immediately lose the sense of the cause of our success. But, after dwelling awhile on our new happiness, we verify all the incidents that have produced it, and the examination of each of them separately still further enhances our satisfaction. It is our present purpose to develop fully the reasons why our readers should participate in our enjoyment.

271

All French citizens have joined in celebrating the downfall of Royalty and the creation of a Republic, yet, among those who applaud, there are some persons who have not an entirely clear comprehension of their former situation or of that upon which they are now entering.

All Frenchmen have shuddered at the perjuries of the King, the plots of his Court and the profligacy of his brothers; so that the race of Louis was deposed from the throne of their hearts long before it was deposed by legislative decree. We do not effect much, however, if we merely dethrone an idol; we must also break to pieces the pedestal upon which it rested. It is the office of royalty rather than the holder of the office that is fatal in its consequences. But everyone has not a vivid conception of this fact.

Yet all Frenchmen should be able in the present conjuncture to prove the absurdity of Royalty and the reasonableness of a Republic, whenever these forms of government are discussed; because if you now enjoy freedom and happiness, you should be conscious of the reasons for your contentment.

As a distinction is drawn frequently between Royalty and Monarchy, we had better examine into the question of the pertinency of this distinction.

ROYALTY

The system of Royalty has begun in the same fashion in all countries and among all peoples. A band of robbers, gathered together under a leader, throw themselves on a country and make slaves of its people; then they elect their leader king. Next comes another robber chief, who conquers and kills the first, and makes himself king in his stead. After a time, the recollection of all this violence is obliterated, and the successors of the robber are held to reign quite legitimately. They are shrewd enough to confer a few benefits now and then on their subjects; they corrupt those about them, and, to give an air of sanctity to their origin, they devise pedigrees that are purely fictitious; * afterward, they are aided

---

* The following royal genealogy is to be found in the Boston *Investigator's* compilation of Paine's works:

"ROYAL PEDIGREE:—George III, who was the grandson of George II, who was the son of George I, who was the son of the Princess Sophia, who was the sister of William and Mary, who were the daughter and son-in-law of James II, who was the son of Charles I, who was a traitor to his country and decapitated as such, who was the son of James I, who was the son of Mary, who was the sister (sic) of Edward VI, who was the son of Henry VIII, who was the cold-blooded murderer of his wives, and the Promoter of the Protestant religion, who was the son of Henry VII, who slew Richard III, who smothered his nephew, Edward V, who was the son of Edward IV, who with bloody Richard slew Henry VI, who succeeded Henry V, who was the

by the dishonesty of the priests, and religion befriends their usurped power, which will henceforth be regarded as their hereditary possession.

The consequences that flow from Royalty are such as might be expected from its source. The annals of monarchy abound in such hideous wickedness, such horrible cruelties that only by reading them can we form any idea of the baseness of which human nature is capable. The pictures that we there behold of kings and their ministers and courtiers are so horrifying that humanity is forced to turn away from them with a shudder.

And yet what else could be expected? Kings are monsters in the natural order, and what can we expect from monsters but miseries and crimes? Now, what is Monarchy? Whatever effort may have been made to conceal its true nature and to familiarize the people with that hateful term, its real meaning cannot be disguised: it signifies *absolute power vested in a single person*, although that person be a fool, a

son of Henry IV, who was the cousin of Richard II, who was the son (sic) of Edward III, who was the son of Richard (sic) II, who was the son of Edward I, who was the son of Henry III, who was the son of John, who was the brother of Richard I, who was the son of Henry II, who was the son of Matilda, who was the daughter of Henry I, who was the brother of William Rufus, who was the son of William the Conqueror, who was the son of a whore."—*Editor*.

traitor or a tyrant. Do we not outrage national honor when we suggest the possibility of any people being ruled by such a person as I have denoted?

But, apart from the defects of the individual, government by a single person is vicious in itself. A prince is too small a person himself to be capable of governing even the smallest state. What an absurdity it is, then, to believe in his capacity for the government of a great nation!

However, you will say, there have been kings who were men of genius. Granted: but such intelligent rulers have been a greater curse to nations than those who were intellectually deficient. Kings of that class have always been ambitious, and have compelled their subjects to pay dearly for the conquests and *Te-deums* that were celebrated over the land while its inhabitants were dying of hunger. We have only to turn to the career of Louis XIV and of other sovereigns in proof of the truth of this statement.

What, however, of those rulers who have no claim to ability, and who substitute for it the vices that seem inherent in Royalty? We have the following description of them in the *Contrat Social* of J. J. Rousseau: "The men who take the foremost place in monarchies are often simply base marplots, ordinary rogues, mean intriguers. The trivial intellectual qualities that have raised these people to high positions in courts but serve to make more apparent to the public their real insignificance." In a word, the story of all monarchies supplies proof that, while monarchs do nothing, their ministers do nothing but evil.

While Royalty is harmful from its very nature, hereditary Royalty is, in addition, absurd and disgusting. Just think of it! Yonder is a man who claims that he has a hereditary right to rule me! Where did he get it? From his ancestors, he says, and from mine. But how could they give him a right they did not possess? No man has power over posterity. I can no more be the slave of those who went before me than I can of those who now exist. If we returned to life, we could not rob ourselves of the rights acquired in a second existence; still less could we rob posterity of their rights.

A hereditary crown! A throne to be handed over to a successor! Why, it is to treat our posterity as a herd of cattle who are entirely destitute of either rights or will. No more infamous and indecent illusion ever disgraced humanity than that the people is a herd which may be transmitted from one king to another.

From one point of view, we should not, perhaps, censure kings for their savage cruelty, their brutality and their oppressions; it is not they who are in fault; it is hereditary succession: a swamp breeds serpents; hereditary succession breeds oppressors.

The following is the system of logic upon which are founded the claims of Royalty: "I," says the hereditary prince, "owe my authority to my birth; I owe my birth to God; therefore, I owe nothing to men." When he has a subservient minister, he then proceeds to commit all the crimes of which tyranny is capable, and he never has any idea that he is acting wrongfully. We have plenty of evidence of this fact in the history of all countries.

You must also see clearly that there must be an entire absence of sympathy between ruler and people. What renders us kind and humane? Is it not sympathy, the power which I have of putting myself in my neighbor's place? How can a monarch have sympathy? He can never put himself in anybody's place, for the simple reason that he can never be in any place but his own.

A monarch is naturally and preëminently an egotist. We have innumerable proofs which show that such a person is altogether separated from humanity. When Charles II was asked to punish

Lauderdale for his cruelty to the Scots, his reply was: "Lauderdale may have oppressed the Scots, but he has always supported my interests." A frequent expression of Louis XIV was: "If I were to comply with the will of my people, I should not be King." He lost his temper when anyone spoke of the "safety of the State," or "the calamities of the State."

We might not object to the hereditary succession of kings, if we could always be certain that the throne should be occupied by a wise and virtuous prince. If, however, we but consider the character of those who sit on the thrones of Europe at the present hour, what do we discover? We find that the men who fill them are either fools or tyrants or traitors or libertines, and that in some of them are combined all imaginable vices. It would thus seem that nature and destiny have agreed in the present age to supply us with tangible evidence of the atrocious wickedness and folly of Royalty.

Yet, after all, there is nothing distinctive about the present age in this relation. Hereditary succession is so essentially vicious that it is impossible for the people to hope for the advent of a virtuous prince. A person educated in the belief that he has a right to command others is inevitably bound by his surroundings to lose all sense of reason and justice.

In fact, were not this notion of hereditary kings a serious matter, we might feel inclined to laugh at the absurdity of such an institution. We have to imagine that, as in the case of racehorses, a prince has certain peculiar characteristics that destine him for the throne, just as the courser has certain physical qualities which destine him for the race-track. But in the case of the noble race of Andalusian steeds, certain precautions are taken to insure its genuineness. Surely, in the case of princes, except similar precautions are adopted, no matter how much they violate the laws of decency, it is impossible to discover whether the offspring of a queen is a legitimate prince or a bastard.

Everything connected with hereditary Royalty bears the mark of infamy or folly. Just consider: a person cannot be a mere workman without some sort of ability; to be a king all that a man requires is to be born. The story told by Montaigne of the dog Barkouf who was appointed governor of a province by an Asiatic monarch, excites our amusement. We laugh at the folly of the Egyptians, who set up a pebble on a throne and acknowledged it as their King. But a pebble or a dog would be less harmful to the people who bowed before them than are kings to the nations that pay them servile homage.

An irrational animal or a piece of lifeless rock is less dangerous to a nation than a human idol. Hardly a single example can be adduced where a man of genius has left behind him children worthy of their parentage. And yet the authority vested in a sovereign, must descend to his son! It is like saying that a wise father always has a wise son! A good governor by inheritance is as likely as a good author by inheritance.

Common sense, therefore, is as much outraged by the idea of Royalty as common right is. Still, it is more than an absurdity; it is a plague, because a nation that prostrates itself in presences of an absurdity is degraded. Can that people which reveres equally vice and virtue, ignorance and wisdom, ever have the capacity for managing important affairs? For this reason, it will be noticed that the inhabitants of a monarchical country are often intellectually degenerate and are distinguished for their servile disposition.

Another consequence of this baleful institution is that it destroys equality and introduces what is called "Nobility." Evil a thing as Nobility is, it is less so than government by inheritance. All that the noble asks of me is that I recognize his superiority because of his birth, while the King requires my submission: I am amused by the noble; I feel like setting my foot upon the King.

It was thought that when the Convention voted the abolition of Royalty, some one would speak in its favor. In this relation, a certain philosopher, who believed that no decree should be issued without a preliminary discussion of the question, moved for the appointment of an orator who should bring forward all the arguments that could be adduced in favor of Royalty, so that everything that could be said in its justification should be made clear to the world. It was on the principle that counsel is assigned to the defense, no matter how strong is the evidence of the prisoner's guilt. In the Republic of Venice there was an official whose function it was to assail all testimony, however indisputable. Royalty, however, has plenty of defenders. It is only fitting that we should examine the cogency of their arguments.

1. *The people need a King to protect them from the tyranny of the powerful.*

Let the Rights of Man be established, Equality enthroned, a sound Constitution drafted, with its powers clearly defined; let all privileges, distinctions of birth and monopolies be annulled; establish liberty of trade and industry, the freedom of the press, equal division of family inheritances, publicity of all government measures, and you will be certain to have excellent laws, and may dispel from your mind the dread of the powerful; for, whether they like it or not, all citizens will then be subject to the law.

2. *A King will prevent the Legislature from usurping authority.*

If representatives, who cannot act as administrators or judges, are often renewed, if their functions are determined by law, if the people can summon at any moment their national conventions and primary assemblies, the tyranny of a legislature would have only a very short existence, especially among a people capable of self-defense, who can read, and have newspapers, guns and pikes. Why assume an evil solely for the purpose of providing a remedy?

3. *To strengthen the executive power, we should have a King.*

Such a proposition might have a certain force when we had nobles, priests, parliaments, and other privileged classes. Now, however, the law is all powerful, and as it is the expression of the general will, it is the interest of everyone to see that it is executed. On the contrary, the presence of a hereditary king tends to weaken the executive power, as was clearly demonstrated recently when we attempted to unite Royalty and Liberty in marriage bonds.

For that matter, those who hold this opinion are persons who identify the king with the Executive Power. My readers, I fancy, entertain more enlightened sentiments.

The following is another not uncommon fallacy: "We must have either an hereditary chief or an elective chief. If we have an elective chief, the citizens will quarrel about the candidates, and every election will be followed by a civil war." In the first place, such civil wars as have arisen in England and France were the result, not of election, but of hereditary succession; and, in addition, the scourge of foreign war has, for a score of times, devastated these kingdoms, because of the claims asserted by certain royal families. In fine, all the disturbances that occurred during the Regency had their source in hereditary succession.

The great point, however, to be considered is this: an elective chief will not be followed by a train of courtiers, will not be surrounded with royal pageantry, will not be puffed up with servile adulation, and will not have an income of thirty millions; and besides, his fellow-citizens will not elect him to an office of several years' duration without limiting his authority and keeping his income within due bounds.

Moreover, the presence of a king entails the presence of an aristocracy and of taxation reaching thirty millions. This is doubtless why Franklin styled Royalism *a crime as bad as poisoning*.

The sole reason why Royalty, with all its visionary splendor, its assumed necessity, the superstitious idolatry that follows in its train, was created was for the purpose of exacting from its victims excessive taxation and willing submission.

Royalty and Popery have had the same goal to attain and have been supported by the same deceptions; they are now falling into the same decay under the rays of the same Light.

TO THE ENGLISH ATTORNEY-GENERAL, ON THE PROSECUTION AGAINST THE SECOND PART OF RIGHTS OF MAN

PAINE wrote this letter in Paris, November 11, 1792, to Sir Archibald Macdonald, who represented the British Government in the prosecution of the author of the "Rights of Man" for libel. The Attorney-General read it to the jury at the trial of Paine, December 18 following, which resulted in his being outlawed. In addressing the jury he stated that "If I succeed in this prosecution, he [Paine] shall never return to this country otherwise than 'in vinculis,' for I will outlaw him."

Repeating Paine's phrase, "Mr. Guelph and his profligate sons," the Attorney-General exclaimed to the jury, "This passage is contemptuous, scandalous, false, cruel. Why, gentlemen, is Mr. Paine, in addition to the political doctrines he is teaching us in this country, to teach us the morality and religion of implacability?" Paine's counsel objected vainly to having this letter read, as containing matter likely to divert the jury from the subject of prosecution, the book. Lord Kenyon, the presiding judge, overruled the objection.

SIR:—As there can be no personal resentment between two strangers, I write this letter to you, as to a man against whom I have no animosity.

You have, as Attorney-General, commenced a prosecution against me as the author of "Rights of Man." Had not my duty, in consequence of my being elected a member of the National Convention of France, called me from England, I should have stayed to have contested the injustice of that prosecution; not upon my own account, for I cared not about the prosecution, but to have defended the principles I had advanced in the work.

The duty I am now engaged in is of too much importance to permit me to trouble myself about your prosecution: when I have leisure, I shall have no objection to meet you on that ground; but, as I now stand, whether you go on with the prosecution, or whether you do not, or whether you obtain a verdict, or not, is a matter of the most perfect indifference to me as an individual. If you obtain one (which you are welcome to if you can get it), it cannot affect me either in person, property, or reputation, otherwise than to increase the latter; and with respect to yourself, it is as consistent that you obtain a verdict against the Man in the Moon as against me; neither do I see how you can continue the prosecution against me as you would have done against one of *your own people,* who had absented himself because he was prosecuted; what passed at Dover proves that my departure from England was no secret.

My necessary absence from your country affords the opportunity of knowing whether the prosecution was intended against Thomas Paine, or against the right of the people of England to investigate systems and principles of government; for as I cannot now be the object of the prosecution, the going on with the prosecution will show that something else was the object, and that something else can be no other than the people of England, for it is against *their rights,* and not against me, that a verdict or sentence can operate, if it can operate at all.   Be then so candid as to tell the jury (if you choose to continue the process), whom it is you are prosecuting, and on whom it is that the verdict is to fall.

But I have other reasons than those I have mentioned for writing you this letter; and, however you may choose to interpret them, they proceed from a good heart.   The time, Sir, is becoming too serious to play with court prosecutions, and sport with national rights.   The terrible examples that have taken place here, upon men who, less than a year ago, thought themselves as secure as any prosecuting judge, jury, or attorney-general, now can in England, ought to have some weight with men in your situation.

That the Government of England is as great, if not the greatest, perfection of fraud and corruption that ever took place since governments began, is what you cannot be a stranger to, unless the constant habit of seeing it has blinded your senses; but though you may not choose to see it, the people are seeing it very fast, and the progress is beyond what you may choose to believe.   Is it possible that you or I can believe, or that reason can make any other man believe, that the capacity of such a man as Mr. Guelph, or any of his profligate sons, is necessary to the government of a nation? I speak to you as one man ought to speak to another; and I know also that I speak what other people are beginning to think.

That you cannot obtain a verdict (and if you do, it will signify nothing) without *packing a jury* (and we *both* know that such tricks are practised), is what I have very good reason to believe. I have gone into coffee-houses, and places where I was unknown, on purpose to learn the currency of opinion, and I never yet saw any company of twelve men that condemned the book; but I have often found a greater number than twelve approving it, and this I think is *a fair way of collecting the natural currency of opinion*.

Do not then, Sir, be the instrument of drawing twelve men into a situation that may be *injurious* to them afterwards. I do not speak this from policy, but from benevolence; but if you choose to go on with the process, I make it my request to you that you will read this letter in court, after which the judge and the jury may do as they please. As I do not consider myself the object of the prosecution, neither can I be affected by the issue, one way or the other, I shall, though a foreigner in your country, subscribe as much money as any other man toward supporting the right of the nation against the prosecution; and it is for this purpose only that I shall do it.

THOMAS PAINE.

As I have not time to copy letters, you will excuse the corrections.

P. S.—I intended, had I stayed in England, to have published the information, with my remarks upon it, before the trial came on; but as I am otherwise engaged, I reserve myself till the trial is over when I shall reply fully to everything you shall advance.

ON THE PROPRIETY OF BRINGING LOUIS XVI
TO TRIAL

HAVING written this address in English on November 20, 1792, Paine caused it to be translated and read to the French National Convention, to which he was a delegate, on the following day. The French poet-statesman Lamartine has admonished Paine for this address; but the trial of Louis XVI was a foregone conclusion, and Paine was already trying to avert popular fury from Louis himself by directing it against the monarchical system. Nor would his subsequent plea for the King's life have been listened to but for this earlier address.

Such statements as "Everybody knows that the Landgrave of Hesse [employed by the English Crown] fights only as far as he is paid . . . and if the trial of Louis XVI could bring it to light that this detestable dealer in human flesh has been paid with the produce of the taxes imposed on the English people, it would be justice to that nation to disclose that fact," precluded the publication of this address in England.

AS I do not know precisely what day the Convention will resume the discussion on the trial of Louis XVI, and, on account of my inability to express myself in French, I cannot speak at the tribune, I request permission to deposit in your hands the inclosed paper, which contains my opinion on that subject. I make this demand with so much eagerness, because circumstances will prove how much it imports to France, that Louis XVI should continue to enjoy good health. I should be happy if the Convention would have the goodness to hear this paper read this morning, as I propose sending a copy of it to London, to be printed in the English journals.

THOMAS PAINE.

A secretary read the opinion of Thomas Paine.

I think it necessary that Louis XVI should be tried; not that this advice is suggested by a spirit of vengeance, but because this measure appears to me just, lawful, and conformable to sound policy. If Louis is innocent, let us put him to prove his innocence; if he is guilty, let the national will determine whether he shall be pardoned or punished.

But besides the motives personal to Louis XVI, there are others which make his trial necessary. I am about to develop these motives, in the language which I think expresses them, and no other. I forbid myself the use of equivocal expression or of mere ceremony.

There was formed among the crowned brigands of Europe a conspiracy which threatened not only French liberty, but likewise that of all nations. Everything tends to the belief that Louis XVI was the partner of this horde of conspirators. You have this man in your power, and he is at present the only one of the band of whom you can make sure. I consider Louis XVI in the same point of view as the two first robbers taken up in the affair of the Store Room; their trial led to discovery of the gang to which they belonged.

We have seen the unhappy soldiers of Austria, of Prussia, and the other powers which declared themselves our enemies, torn from their fire-sides, and drawn to butchery like wretched animals, to sustain, at the cost of their blood, the common cause of these crowned brigands. They loaded the inhabitants of those regions with taxes to support the expenses of the war. All this was not done solely for Louis XVI. Some of the conspirators have acted openly: but there is reason to presume that this conspiracy is composed of two classes of brigands; those who have taken up arms, and those who have lent to their cause secret encouragement and clandestine assistance. Now it is indispensable to let France and the whole world know all these accomplices.

A little time after the National Convention was constituted, the Minister for Foreign Affairs presented the picture of all the governments of Europe —those whose hostilities were public, and those that acted with a mysterious circumspection. This picture supplied grounds for just suspicions of the part the latter were disposed to take, and since then various circumstances have occurred to confirm those suspicions.

We have already penetrated into some part of the conduct of Mr. Guelph, Elector of Hanover, and strong presumptions involve the same man, his Court and ministers, in quality of King of England. M. Calonne has constantly been favored with a friendly reception at that Court. The arrival of Mr. Smith, secretary to Mr. Pitt, at Coblentz, when the emigrants were assembling there; the recall of the English Ambassador; the extravagant joy manifested by the Court of St. James's at the false report of the defeat of Dumouriez, when it was communicated by Lord Elgin, then Minister of Great Britain at Brussels— all these circumstances render him [George III] extremely suspicious; the trial of Louis XVI will probably furnish more decisive proofs.

The long subsisting fear of a revolution in England, would alone, I believe, prevent that court from manifesting as much publicity in its operations as Austria and Prussia. Another reason could be added to this: The inevitable decrease of credit, by means of which alone all the old governments could obtain fresh loans, in proportion as the probability of revolutions increased. Whoever invests in the new loans of such governments must expect to lose his stock.

Everybody knows that the Landgrave of Hesse fights only as far as he is paid. He has been for many years in the pay of the Court of London. If the trial of Louis XVI could bring it to light that this detestable dealer in human flesh has been paid with the produce of the taxes imposed on the English people, it would be justice to that nation to disclose that fact. It would at the same time give to France an exact knowledge of the character of that court, which has not ceased to be the most intriguing in Europe, ever since its connection with Germany.

Louis XVI considered as an individual, is an object beneath the notice of the Republic; but when he is looked upon as a part of that band of conspirators, as an accused man whose trial may lead all nations in the world to know and detest the disastrous system of monarchy, and the plots and intrigues of their own courts, he ought to be tried.

If the crimes for which Louis XVI is arraigned were absolutely personal to him, without reference to general conspiracies, and confined to the affairs of France, the plea of inviolability, that folly of the moment, might have been urged in his behalf with some appearance of reason; but he is arraigned not only for treasons against France, but for having conspired against all Europe, and if France is to be just to all Europe we ought to use every means in our power to discover the whole extent of that conspiracy.

France is now a Republic; she has completed her revolution; but she cannot earn all its advantages so long as she is surrounded with despotic governments. Their armies and their marine oblige her also to keep troops and ships in readiness. It is therefore her immediate interest that all nations shall be as free as herself; that revolutions shall be universal; and since the trial of Louis XVI can serve to prove to the world the flagitiousness of governments in general, and the necessity of revolutions, she ought not to let slip so precious an opportunity.

The despots of Europe have formed alliances to preserve their respective authority, and to perpetuate the oppression of peoples. This is the end they proposed to themselves in their invasion of French territory. They dread the effect of the French Revolution in the bosom of their own countries; and in hopes of preventing it, they are come to attempt the destruction of this revolution before it should attain its perfect maturity. Their attempt has not been attended with success. France has already vanquished their armies; but it remains for her to sound the particulars of the conspiracy, to discover, to expose to the eyes of the world, those despots who had the infamy to take part in it; and the world expects from her that act of justice.

These are my motives for demanding that Louis XVI be judged; and it is in this sole point of view that his trial appears to me of sufficient importance to receive the attention of the Republic.

As to "inviolability," I would not have such a word mentioned. If, seeing in Louis XVI only a weak and narrow-minded man, badly reared, like all his kind, given, as it is said, to frequent excesses of drunkenness—a man whom the National Assembly imprudently raised again on a throne for which he was not made—he is shown hereafter some compassion, it shall be the result of the national magnanimity, and not the burlesque notion of a pretended "inviolability."

THOMAS PAINE.

REASONS FOR PRESERVING THE LIFE OF LOUIS CAPET

A FRENCH translation of this address was read to the National Convention, January 15, 1793, Paine's mastery of the French language being limited. It will be noted that the author of the "Rights of Man," of "Common Sense" and of "The American Crisis" urges that Louis XVI be given an asylum in America "far removed from the miseries and crimes of royalty."

Later on, while Paine was in prison for ten months in Paris, he was accused in England and America of having speeded the death of Louis XVI. A preface to the 1796 publication in England of this address describes it as "a burnt offering to Truth, in behalf of the most zealous friend and advocate of the Rights of Man; to protect him against the barbarous shafts of scandal and delusion, as a reply to all the horrors which despots of every description have, with such unrelenting malice, attempted to fix on his conduct."

CITIZEN PRESIDENT: My hatred and abhorrence of monarchy are sufficiently known: they originate in principles of reason and conviction, nor, except with life, can they ever be extirpated; but my compassion for the unfortunate, whether friend or enemy, is equally lively and sincere.

I voted that Louis should be tried, because it was necessary to afford proofs to the world of the perfidy, corruption and abomination of the monarchical system. The infinity of evidence that has been produced exposes them in the most glaring and hideous colors; thence it results that monarchy, whatever form it may assume, arbitrary or otherwise, becomes necessarily a center round which are united every species of corruption, and the kingly trade is no less destructive of all morality in the human breast, than the trade of an executioner is destructive of its sensibility. I remember, during my residence in another country, that I was exceedingly struck with a sentence of M. Autheine at the Jacobins [Club], which corresponds exactly with my own idea —"Make me a king to-day," said he, "and I shall be a robber to-morrow."

Nevertheless, I am inclined to believe that if Louis Capet had been born in obscure condition, had he lived within the circle of an amiable and respectable neighborhood, at liberty to practise the duties of domestic life, had he been thus situated, I cannot believe that he would have shown himself destitute of social virtues; we are, in a moment of fermentation like this, naturally little indulgent to his vices, or rather to those of his government; we regard them with additional horror and indignation; not that they are more heinous than those of his predecessors, but because our eyes are now open, and the veil of delusion at length withdrawn; yet the lamentable, degraded state to which he is actually reduced, is surely far less imputable to him than to the Constituent

Assembly, which, of its own authority, without consent or advice of the people, restored him to the throne.

I was in Paris at the time of the flight, or abdication of Louis XVI, and when he was taken and brought back. The proposal of restoring him to supreme power struck me with amazement; and although at that time I was not a French citizen, yet as a citizen of the world I employed all the efforts that depended on me to prevent it.

A small society, composed only of five persons, two of whom are now members of the Convention, took at that time the name of the Republican Club (Société Républicaine). This society opposed the restoration of Louis, not so much on account of his personal offenses, as in order to overthrow the monarchy, and to erect on its ruins the republican system and an equal representation.

With this design, I traced out in the English language certain propositions, which were translated with some trifling alterations, and signed by Achille Duchâtelet, now Lieutenant-General in the army of the French Republic, and at that time one of the five members which composed our little party: the law requiring the signature of a citizen at the bottom of each printed paper.

The paper was indignantly torn by Malouet; and brought forth in this very room as an article of accusation against the person who had signed it, the author and their adherents; but such is the revolution of events, that this paper is now received and brought forth for a very opposite purpose—to remind the nation of the errors of that unfortunate day, that fatal error of not having then banished Louis XVI from its bosom, and to plead this day in favor of his exile, preferable to his death. The paper in question was conceived in the following terms: [See "A Republican Manifesto."]

Having thus explained the principles and the exertions of the republicans at that fatal period, when Louis was reinstated in full possession of the executive power which by his flight had been suspended, I return to the subject, and to the deplorable situation in which the man is now actually involved.

What was neglected at the time of which I have been speaking, has been since brought about by the force of necessity. The wilful, treacherous defects in the former Constitution have been brought to light; the continual alarm of treason and conspiracy aroused the nation, and produced eventually a second revolution. The people have beat down, royalty, never, never to rise again; they have brought Louis

Capet to the bar, and demonstrated in the face of the whole world, the intrigues, the cabals, the falsehood, corruption, and rooted depravity, the inevitable effects of monarchical government.   There remains then only one question to be considered, what is to be done with this man?

For myself I seriously confess, that when I reflect on the unaccountable folly that restored the executive power to his hands, all covered as he was with perjuries and treason, I am far more ready to condemn the Constituent Assembly than the unfortunate prisoner Louis Capet.

But abstracted from every other consideration, there is one circumstance in his life which ought to cover or at least to palliate a great number of his transgressions, and this very circumstance affords to the French nation a blessed occasion of extricating itself from the yoke of kings, without defiling itself in the impurities of their blood.

It is to France alone, I know, that the United States of America owe that support which enabled them to shake off the unjust and tyrannical yoke of Britain.   The ardor and zeal which she displayed to provide both men and money, were the natural consequence of a thirst for liberty.   But as the nation at that time, restrained by the shackles of her own government, could only act by the means of a monarchical organ, this organ—whatever in other respects the object might be—certainly performed a good, a great action.

Let then those United States be the safeguard and asylum of Louis Capet. There, hereafter, far removed from the miseries and crimes of royalty, he may learn, from the constant aspect of public prosperity, that the true system of government consists not in kings, but in fair, equal and honorable representation.

In relating this circumstance, and in submitting this proposition, I consider myself as a citizen of both countries. I submit it as a citizen of America, who feels the debt of gratitude which he owes to every Frenchman. I submit it also as a man, who, although the enemy of kings, cannot forget that they are subject to human frailties. I support my proposition as a citizen of the French Republic, because it appears to me the best, the most politic measure that can be adopted.

As far as my experience in public life extends, I have ever observed, that the great mass of the people are invariably just, both in their intentions and in their objects; but the true method of accomplishing an effect does not always show itself in the first instance. For example; the English nation had groaned under the despotism of the Stuarts. Hence Charles I lost his life; yet Charles II was restored to all the plentitude of power, which his father had lost. Forty years had not expired when the same family strove to re-establish their ancient oppression; so the nation then banished from its territories the whole race. The remedy was effectual. The Stuart family sank into obscurity, confounded itself with the multitude, and is at length extinct.

The French nation has carried her measures of government to a greater length. France is not satisfied with exposing the guilt of the monarch. She has penetrated into the vices and horrors of the monarchy. She has shown them clear as daylight, and forever crushed that system; and he, whoever he may be, that should ever dare to reclaim those rights would be regarded not as a pretender, but punished as a traitor.

Two brothers of Louis Capet have banished themselves from the country; but they are obliged to comply with the spirit and etiquette of the courts where they reside. They can advance no pretensions on their own account, so long as Louis Capet shall live.

Monarchy, in France, was a system pregnant with crime and murders, cancelling all natural ties, even those by which brothers are united. We know how often they have assassinated each other to pave a way to power. As those hopes which the emigrants had reposed in Louis XVI, are fled, the last that remains rests upon his death, and their situation inclines them to desire this catastrophe, that they may once again rally around a more active chief, and try one further effort under the fortune of the ci-devant Monsieur and D' Artois. That such an enterprise would precipitate them into a new abyss of calamity and disgrace, it is not difficult to foresee; yet it might be attended with mutual loss, and it is our duty as legislators not to spill a drop of blood when our purpose may be effectually accomplished without it.

It has already been proposed to abolish the punishment of death, and it is with infinite satisfaction that I recollect the humane and excellent oration pronounced by Robespierre on that subject in the Constituent Assembly. This cause must find its advocates in every corner where enlightened politicians and lovers of humanity exist, and it ought above all to find them in this assembly.

Monarchical governments have trained the human race, and inured it to the sanguinary arts and refinements of punishment; and it is exactly the same punishment which has so long shocked the sight and tormented the patience of the people, that now, in their turn, they practise in revenge upon their oppressors. But it becomes us to be strictly on our guard against the abomination and perversity of monarchical examples: as France has been the first of European nations to abolish royalty, let her also be the first to abolish the punishment of death, and to find out a milder and more effectual substitute.

In the particular case now under consideration, I submit the following propositions: 1st, That the National Convention shall pronounce sentence of banishment on Louis and his family, 2d, That Louis Capet shall be detained in prison till the end of the war, and at that epoch the sentence of banishment to be executed.

SHALL LOUIS XVI BE RESPITED?

PAINE, who was not an orator and who could not speak French fluently, deputized a fellow member of the French National Convention named Bancal to translate and read this address of his, January 19, 1793. It is taken from contemporary French reports, which also state that when Paine voted against submitting the fate of Louis XVI to a popular vote, it was believed that the King's doom was sealed.

Gouverneur Morris, the American Minister to France, who was in close touch with the King, had written to President Washington on January 6, 1793: "The King's fate is to be decided next Monday, the 14th. That unhappy man, conversing with one of his counsel, calmly summed up the motives of every kind, and concluded that a majority of the council would vote for referring his case to the people, and that in consequence he should be massacred." Writing to Washington nine days earlier, Morris quotes Paine as saying that he planned to move the banishment of Louis XVI and Marie Antoinette to America.

THE decision come to in the Convention yesterday in favor of death has filled me with genuine sorrow—

Marat (interrupting) —I deny the right of Thomas Paine to vote on such a subject; as he is a Quaker, of course his religious views run counter to the infliction of capital punishment. *(There is considerable disorder, which, however, is allayed by shouts for "free speech." Then Bancal continues the reading of the translation.)*

I may lay claim to the possession of a certain amount of experience; I have taken no inconsiderable part in the struggle for freedom during the Revolution of the United

States of America: it is a cause to which I have devoted almost twenty years of my existence. Liberty
and humanity have ever been the words that best
expressed my thoughts, and it is my conviction that
the union of these two principles, in all cases, tends
more than anything also to insure the grandeur of a
nation. I am aware of the excitement and anger
aroused by the perils to which France, and especially
Paris, have been subjected; and yet, if we could only
catch a glimpse of the future, long after all this excitement and anger have passed away, it is not un-
likely that the action which you have sanctioned to-
day will assume the aspect of having been performed
from a spirit of revenge rather than from a spirit of
justice. (*Murmurs.*) My solicitude for the welfare
of France has now been transformed into concern for
her honor.

Should I, after returning to America, spend my
leisure in writing a history of the French Revolution,
it would give me greater satisfaction to be able to set
down a multitude of mistakes prompted by a feeling
of compassion rather than to record a single deed
prompted by even a just severity. I voted against
the resolution that the Convention should submit its
judgment to the decision of the people; I did so, how-

ever, in the expectation that it would not decide in favor of death, but rather in favor of a penalty for which I believe the nation would have voted; namely, imprisonment during the war and exile afterward. Such a punishment, embracing as it would the whole family, would be more effective than any other that can be imagined.

I have not altered my views as to the undesirability of leaving the punishment to the decision of the primary assemblies, for I consider that there is a better method of dealing with the matter. The Convention has been chosen in order that it may establish a constitution, which constitution must be subsequently ratified by the primary assemblies. As a necessary consequence, another assembly must then be elected. Now, it is not probable that the Convention now sitting can continue for more than five or six months.

The selection that shall be made of the new deputies will voice the opinion of the people as strongly on the justice of your sentence as would the result of an appeal to the primary assemblies. As then, our functions must soon terminate, we should be careful to pay due regard to the welfare of those who shall succeed us. We should not, by adopting measures calculated to enlarge the number of our enemies or to reduce that of our friends—especially when our financial position may be worse than it is to-day—place difficulties in the path of the latter. Let us not, therefore, decide any question hastily or rashly.

France's sole ally is the United States of America. It is the only nation upon which France can depend for a supply of naval stores, because all the kingdoms of northern Europe are either now waging war against her, or shortly will be. Now, it is an unfortunate circumstance that the individual whose fate we are at present determining has always been regarded by the people of the United States as a friend to their own revolution. Should you come, then, to the resolution of putting Louis to death, you will excite the heart-felt sorrow of your ally. If I were able to speak the French language, I would appear in person at your bar, and, in the name of the American people, ask that Louis be respited—

Thuriot—The words you are reading are not those of Thomas Paine.

Marat—I denounce the translator. Such opinions are not Thomas Paine's. The translation is incorrect.

Garran—It is a correct translation of the original, which I have read.

(*Great confusion, Paine ascends the tribune and, standing beside Bancal, declares that the opinions just delivered are his own.*)

Bancal continues to read the translation:

It is my fondest desire that when an ambassador has been sent by your executive committee to Philadelphia, he may carry with him the tidings from France of the respite granted by the National Convention to Louis, solely because of its friendship for America. In the name of the citizens of that Republic, I beg that you delay the execution. Do not, I beseech you, bestow upon the English tyrant the satisfaction of learning that the man who helped America, the land of my love, to burst her fetters, has died on the scaffold.

Marat (rushing into the middle of the chamber) —Paine's reason for voting against the death penalty is that he is a Quaker.

Paine—I have been influenced in my vote by public policy as well as by moral reasons.

PLAN OF A DECLARATION

Of the Natural, Civil and Political Rights of Man

APPEALING to the French National Convention from the Luxembourg prison, where he was confined during most of the year 1794, Paine states that, as a member of the committee for framing the Constitution, he had prepared a Plan, probably in collaboration with Condorcet, from whose works the accompanying document is taken. This is corroborated by Dr. John Moore, in whose "Aphorisms, Opinions and Reflections of Thomas Paine" (London, 1826) it is stated that such a collaboration occurred.

As the Constitution of 1793 was reported by the Committee on February 15, and as Robespierre objected to the "Declaration of Rights" on April 15 because it made no mention of a Supreme Being, it must have been drawn up before those dates, probably in January. Jefferson regretted with Paine that the Constitution of the United States contained no Declaration of Rights to safeguard the individual against a despotic majority.

THE aim of men gathered together in society being the maintenance of their natural, civil and political rights, these rights are the basis of the social compact, and their recognition and their declaration should precede the constitution which assures their guarantee.

1. The natural, civil and political rights of man are liberty, equality, security, property, social guarantees, and resistance to oppression.

2. Liberty is the power to do everything that does not interfere with the rights of others: thus, the exercise of the natural rights of every indi-

315

vidual has no limits save those that assure to other members of society the enjoyment of the same rights.

3. The preservation of liberty depends on obedience to the law, which is the expression of the general will. Anything that is not prohibited by the law cannot be forbidden, and no one can be constrained to do that which the law does not ordain.

4. Every man is free to publish his thoughts and opinions.

5. The freedom of the press, and of every other medium for the expression of thought, cannot be interdicted, suspended or limited.

6. Every man is free in the exercise of his religion.

7. Equality consists in the enjoyment of the same rights by each.

8. The law should be equal for all, whether it rewards or punishes, whether it protects or restrains.

9. All citizens have the right of admission to all public positions, employments and functions. The only motives of preference known to a free people are talents and virtues.

10. Security consists in the protection granted by society to every citizen for the preservation of his person, his possessions and his rights.

11. No one should be summoned before a court, arrested, accused or imprisoned except in cases deter-

mined by law, and according to the forms which it prescribes. All other acts directed against a citizen are arbitrary and null.

12. Those who solicit, assist, sign, execute or cause to be executed such acts, are criminals and should be punished.

13. Citizens exposed to such acts have the right to repel force by force; but every citizen, summoned or arrested by the authority of the law, and according to the forms prescribed by the law, should at once submit: he is culpable if he resist.

14. As every man is presumed to be innocent until he is proved to be guilty, all rigor that is not needed for the security of his person should be severely checked by the law, in case of his arrest.

15. No one should be punished save by a law enacted and promulgated anteriorly to the crime, and legally applied.

16. A law that punishes crimes committed before its existence, is an act of despotism, because a retroactive effect given to a law as in itself a crime.

17. The law should not decree any penalties that are not strictly and evidently necessary for the general safety. The punishment should fit the crime and be useful to society.

18. The right of property consists in the liberty of every man to make such a disposition of his possessions, capital, income and industry as he chooses.

19. No citizen can be prevented from engaging in any kind of labor, commerce or agriculture; he can manufacture, sell and transport every species of production.

20. Every man can pledge his services and his time; but he cannot sell himself: his person is not an alienable property.

21. No one can be deprived of the smallest portion of his property without his own consent, except when a public need, legally established, plainly requires it, and then only on condition of a just, preliminary indemnity.

22. No tax can be exacted save for the general utility and for the purpose of relieving the public necessities. All citizens have the right of assenting, either in person or by the representatives, to the imposition of taxes.

23. Education is the right of everyone, and society owes it to all its members equally.

24. To aid the needy is a sacred debt of society; and it is for the law to determine its extent and application.

25. The social guarantee of the rights of man is based upon the national sovereignty.

26. The national sovereignty is one, indivisible, imprescriptible and inalienable.

27. It resides essentially in the entire people, and each citizen has an equal right to concur in its exercise.

28. No partial assembly of citizens and no individual, can be invested with this sovereignty, or can exercise any authority or fulfil any public function without the formal delegation of the law.

29. The social guarantee cannot exist if the limits of public functions are not clearly determined by the law, and if the responsibility of all public functionaries is not assured.

30. All citizens are bound to concur in this guarantee, and to assist the law, when they are summoned in its name.

31. Men, gathered together in society, should have the legal means of resisting oppression.

32. There is oppression when a law violates the natural, civil or political rights which it ought to guarantee. There is oppression when the law is violated by public functionaries in its application to individual acts. There is oppression when arbitrary acts, opposed to the expression, of the law, violate

the rights of citizens. In every free government, the method of resistance to these various acts of oppression should be regulated by the constitution.

33. A people has always the right to review, reform and change its constitution. One generation has not the right to subject future generations to its laws; and all heredity in public employments is absurd and tyrannical.